STEPPING BEYOND KHAKI

STEPPING BEYOND KHAKI

Revelations of A Real-Life Singham

K. Annamalai

BLOOMSBURY

NEW DELHI • LONDON • OXFORD • NEW YORK • SYDNEY

BLOOMSBURY INDIA
Bloomsbury Publishing India Pvt. Ltd
Second Floor, LSC Building No. 4, DDA Complex, Pocket C – 6 & 7,
Vasant Kunj, New Delhi 110070

BLOOMSBURY, BLOOMSBURY INDIA and the Diana logo are trademarks of Bloomsbury Publishing Plc

First published in India 2021
This edition published in 2021

ISBN: PB: 978-93-89449-85-3; eBook: 978-93-89449-87-7

8 10 9 7

Typeset in Manipal Technologies Limited
Printed and bound in India by Replika Press Pvt. Ltd.

To

All the men and women who had worn khaki and made themselves worthy of it

CONTENTS

THE FACELESS HEROES

GAME CHANGERS

FOREWORD

The author had a brief but brilliant innings with the Indian Police Service, blazing a trail wherever he served. The reasons for his successes as well as the triggers for his quitting a service that he dearly loved, come out clearly through this book. Each chapter is unique and worth reading. The narration is very simple, interesting and the flow takes us easily from his school days to his last official position as Superintendent of Police, gradually maturing from an unknown to a respected police officer. His empathy is self-evident in the simple but gripping anecdotes that dot this book. In simple prose, he takes the reader on a guided tour of policing—a world whose gamut, naturally, spans all of society's echelons, from scum to the elite, encompassing within it all citizens who crave fairness and justice. How the author balances all these with dignity and self-esteem, is edifying. That the emotional quotient clearly counts more than the intelligence quotient is another key takeaway. He touches upon almost all aspects of policing—from dealing with rules and regulations, the public, subordinates, seniors, politicians and last but not least, with the self (as a police officer and as a human being, and the struggle between these two in deciding the right and wrong in a holistic manner). The pages of this book drip with conviction, passion and emotion. Leadership oozes from almost every page.

On leadership the author cites KPS Gill—a doyen of the Indian Police. Legendary EN Rammohan in his book *Simply Khaki* refers to the times of policemen's agitation in Assam. In KPS Gill's jurisdiction there was no trouble. The chorus of agitating policemen's wives was, 'We need more KPS Gills'. That is the measure of a true leader.

A caring leader at every level is what our police forces deserve, for its men are at the frontiers of internal security as its first responders. The current wisdom is that there is scarcely a seam between internal and external security. True, the Indian Police Services, of the States and Centre have many gems in their ranks, gazetted or otherwise. But as the author points out, the systems should be in place to facilitate 'fair policing so that the common man benefits'.

Though most of the straightforward people in the police force may be averse to political interference in policing, in a democracy like India it is an integral part of policing. The author has rightly explained the aspiration of the public from a politician and elucidated on the reasons for tainted politicians overshadowing the righteous ones. He has touched upon the subject of criminalisation in politics and also on the need to understand politicians, their commitments and compulsions. Annamalai's experience in dealing with politicians, his views on them and the tips given by him at the end of the chapter titled 'The Breed of Indian Politicians' will help young IPS officers in learning to deal with politicians without compromising their integrity and responsibility—mastering the art of policing with political balancing. His patience and perseverance in learning the nuances of policing in such a short time is admirable. His policy of policing with a humane touch and his keenness to stick to the right path is worth emulating. Not only politics, but he has also devoted one chapter on government/governance and the need of reforms. His view that 'democracy by its very foundation is not a perfect mechanism to deliver the goods' is worth pondering on.

To a non-policeman, this book offers a peek into the policing world with its good, bad and ugly innards. But mostly, it's the abundance of goodness in selfless men that stands out. To every policeman, this is a must read—anyone commanding upwards of a section of men—whether he is in the State Police or Central Armed Police Forces.

K Vijay Kumar IPS (Retd)
Senior Security Advisor
Ministry of Home Affairs (MHA)
Government of India

ACKNOWLEDGEMENTS

This is a book I believed I would never start or, having started, see through its completion. My ability to write was limited to a few articles for the college magazine and a page for personal diary when I felt like maintaining one. Writing close to 60,000 words for a book really tested me—my patience, my persistence and, most importantly, my ability to focus. More than me sharing my perspectives of life and the circumstances that made me, this was a soul-searching exercise—an exercise that I wouldn't have gone through except for this book. So I treat penning down this book as a unique honour. My special thanks to you, the reader, as you have stayed with me almost till the last leaf.

Considering the changed circumstances of my life post resigning from the Indian Police Service, this book was made possible entirely due to a whole host of people whom I should acknowledge here. Firstly, my wife Akila for being with me and for constantly pushing and encouraging me to complete this book. This was despite her full-time job, managing our son and bringing into this world our beautiful girl, just about when I completed this book. Technically, she should be the co-author for her efforts!

Satish Acharya, a dear friend and a cartoonist whom I deeply respect, agreed to do all the illustrations in this book. Without even allowing me to complete my request, he agreed to do this. Reading my thoughts and converting them into an illustration to capture the essence of each chapter is no mean task and I jokingly told him that some of his illustrations are far better than my chapters. I know, he did this only for our friendship—I'm truly humbled.

I thank my friend Suraj for his critical and unbiased comments, Rajendiran for his unvarnished, honest opinion after reading the manuscript, Lakshmi for looking at the grammar and Shiva Kumar for his constant motivation despite our hectic travel schedule—I hope I have lived up to your time and energy given for this book as if this is yours.

This book was complete for me when a person I deeply admire agreed to write the foreword. Mr K Vijay Kumar, IPS (Retd) and senior security adviser, Ministry of Home Affairs (MHA), agreed to write despite his busy life, honouring a simple message of request from me. A fantastic officer and a human being of the finest quality, he not only wrote the foreword but also proofread my effort—I'm truly blessed.

My publisher, Praveen Tiwari of Bloomsbury, chose to see only the positive part of this whole effort and gently moved me towards the final output. Thanks to him, this book reflects the unpaved road I took along with the bouquets and brickbats that came along. Shreya Chakraborti, Editorial Manager, and Nitin Valecha, Senior Manager, Acquisitions, deserve a loud shout-out for their professionalism and support.

This book is about our everyday heroes—the brave policemen and women who protect and secure us. They are giving their today for our better tomorrow. I thank you all for allowing me to travel a part of my life along with you. Receiving your salute and honouring it with my actions would be the single, greatest privilege of my life.

Why Quit When the Going Is Good?

Like most of you, in my early twenties, I saw my life as a series of obstacles that needed to be conquered; and because of that, I was also a person with confused priorities. The more I came out of my shell and started to see real people and real problems, the more I started seeing life for what it was. My life took a turn for good when I went to the Indian Institute of Management Lucknow for my postgraduate studies. The world of Uttar Pradesh and its hinterlands was far different from my Chennai and Coimbatore. The reality of the world I had seen there shook me. The stark and abject poverty in the hinterlands along with the injustice one human can do to another, took me to another world. It quickly re-ordered my priorities in life and I started searching for ways to make my life more meaningful and purposeful. What started as an internship with a political party in Tamil Nadu in 2009, took me to a civil service life from 2010 onwards, where I was an IPS officer for about nine years, serving the wonderful state of Karnataka. At thirty-five, and hopefully not in the middle of my life yet, I was feeling that inner urge to explore other opportunities as I felt the world of policing had completely taken me into the world of crimes and criminals. Though it was a fantastic time wearing my khaki, I was yearning to move out and to meet some positive people as well. The trip to Kailash in 2018 and the untimely death of a senior officer whom I deeply admired, gave me the final impetus to take that unchartered path.

I'm fully settled in my new phase of life, running a foundation in Tamil Nadu that focuses on creating leaders at grassroots,I never had the idea of writing a book. TN Hari, the head of Human Resources at Big Basket, invited me for a talk at his office in Bengaluru. While conversing with his team members, I found that the policing world is not only unknown to the public but also largely misunderstood by them. After the talk, Hari planted in me the idea of a book while we were in his office elevator and one thing led to another. I unconsciously allowed this seed to grow in my head without understanding the nuances of writing a book and this blind acceptance really tested me. Later, when I attempted to give shape to the book, I understood it is like baring our soul and re-examining it continuously. The process of writing this book has really tested me, exposed to me many of my blind spots, and more importantly, made me humbler. I have written keeping myself in the background, and I can now see how I owe a very large part of my success to those unsung heroes who remain hidden in their uniforms. For me, this was what motivated me to put my pen to paper and brave this ordeal. I believe I have gone deep into the policing world of how perceptions shape us, corruption scuttles our hard earned progress, the daily struggle one faces between Dharma and law along with the unknown world—to most of us—about criminals. I truly believe that the real heroes of the policing world are our beat constables and the officers just above them; in other words, those whose rankings may not be conventionally impressive. I have done my best to bring them out in the open and talk about their heroic work.

A dip into the world of khaki, I'm sure, will throw fresh light on the tough world of policing. Like on our ace investigators, who make sure the culprits are brought to justice and restore our faith in the system; or on the go-getters, who go to any extent to get the job done, most often happily suffering in the process; and on the daily struggles of being a cop. In the last chapter on game changers, I have touched upon some of the much-needed reforms at the political, policing and at governmental level. If you are looking for complete solutions in this book, you might feel disappointed as I tried my best here to open the hidden screen to reveal what is truly happening in the inside. That's the focus of this book.

The real heroes, as I said, in the journey of this book are our constables and other hard working cops. If my face has come out anywhere, please pardon my vanity. Change happens when we are ready for it and this book is an attempt to push us in that direction.

My sincere thanks to you for trusting me and picking up this book. I hope I do justice to your faith.

K Annamalai

THE BEGINNING

A life of respect and honour

The Initial Days

I was born in a village which goes by the name Thottampatti in Karur, Tamil Nadu that taught me everything and pretty much prepared me for the journey of life. A village with about fifty houses in total with all of them predominantly engaged in agriculture. It was an age of small dreams, solitude and routine. With a premium placed on education by my parents, I had to travel a total of 50 kilometres up and down on bicycle and buses for my initial schooling. My parents were very clear that education should take precedence over anything else; they sacrificed their own comforts to put me in an English-medium school at a time and place where it was almost unthinkable to do so. Later, I was sent to a hostel to two different cities to complete my schooling. Like with most kids of my age and background, no big picture emerged for a pretty long time and I just couldn't figure out why I was doing what I was doing. It was a mad rush for passing both the board and the inevitable competitive exams that was the focus of the school and the point of being away from home. The realisation that I had to do something worthwhile and make something out of this life started emerging when I fully settled into my undergraduate studies as an engineering student. Unknowingly, life in the village had taught me everything and more than is required to survive, or even to excel. Like an exercise that builds one's strength fibre by fibre, I suppose life in my village was building up that internal fibre, that quiet strength and moral courage that started coming out during my time in college. Being born into an agricultural family and living in the village taught me to accept life for what it is. My people kept moving ahead even when the rains failed us or when once in a few years, excess rains spoiled the crops. My young mind saw this purely as a success or a failure but for my people this was another test in their daily struggle at the farm. It was also a place where love was genuine, people cared for each other and had all the time for a small conversation. That typical village intimacy around made me very trusting of people and encouraged me to see the best in them. More than the education that I received from some of the finest teachers, it was that village grit and hard work that kept me going in places that were foreign to me and looked to totally overwhelm me.

For me, the realisation of 'what I shouldn't do' came ahead of 'what I should do'. It was very clear to me that working in a software company or in any other corporate set-up was out of the question. I took a year trying to figure out what I should do. This was a risky option for a person like me. In the small world where I grew up, people were judged by what they were doing rather than what they intended to do. There was that extra pressure to get a job and settle down. Life, for most of us in my place, arrived the day we got a job in a big city like Chennai or Bangalore. It, therefore, took me an extra bit of courage to sacrifice a job and search for the unknown. I should thank my mentor, Mr Madhu Nambudri, in Coimbatore who ran an institute to train aspirants for cracking the Common Admission Test (CAT). Countless hours of chatting with him opened up the option of an MBA degree. It looked enticing to me as it was also a safe bet. A master's degree would act as an insurance and I felt it might also help in starting my own business soon. I was also very clear that I might not have the smarts to clear that test but I was very sure that my hard work and grit would see me through. After a year of working towards it with sheer determination, I managed to land myself a seat in the Indian Institute of Management (IIM) Lucknow.

Getting into this world-class institute changed my perspective on life and opened up a world that was far different from the one I had inhabited so far. For the first time in my life, I had seen ultracompetitive individuals bunched together in a place. In the introduction session, I was amazed by the pedigree each one had. Most students perhaps hadn't received anything other than first rank throughout their education. The USP of our elite institutions like IITs and IIMs is that a huge premium is placed on talent and knowledge for selection into them. This attracts a certain group of young minds who crave for competition over anything else. The whole atmosphere was highly charged and with all the running around, I found it very tough to make genuine friends there. As I was observing most of the time, the talks were more about companies visiting the campus or about a life that I felt I wasn't connected with. I witnessed my friends get into that cut-throat world of placements and fat pay cheques. Nothing wrong in what they were doing but luckily it gave me enough time to reflect on and crystalise what I wanted to do in life.

Travelling around Uttar Pradesh, I was able to see a world that was completely different from the southern part of India I grew up in. In our parts, we had a functioning and a reasonably responsible government. The people who I met now, in Lucknow, were unlike my own people with whom I had grown. Better awareness and reasonable education made the people who had been around me thus far to question me when things went wrong and, sadly, I couldn't see the same happening here. They were okay with a bus coming hours late to their bus stop and, many a times, they were just passing their life without an end in sight. No questions were asked when ration shops wouldn't open for days at a time and all they could do was keep visiting the shops daily to see whether that person had come to open it. Education was something like a commodity at a school with no premium on learning and improving themselves. In short, they were living a life that is not far removed from the life that our ancestors lived. At the ground, my eyes were desperately searching for the reason that a person is able to give eight *pooris* for less than twenty Indian rupees. The inquisition was more about why a person is able to afford only that much and the mindset with which he was living. Alternatively, the ingenuity of the person who was able to do it at that cost also intrigued me.

That's also the time I became fascinated with the government and its various roles. The political parties that make up a government, the way elections are conducted and people's voting choices opened up a different world to me. This new found interest kindled in me a fascination for our Indian democracy—one that is not perfect but drives almost all the things in our lives. The more we talk about democracy, its importance and the increasing level of people's awareness, I had met a set of population that was far removed from any government that is operating in a distant area from where they reside. The elected representatives are supposed to be seen once in five years and they are to be seen like Caesar's wife, who is above questioning. It's not that they are above suspicion, but they belong to that elite group who can't be seen, heard or commented upon. This motivated me to explore an internship with a political party during my first year of MBA. I could see the shift happening in me at that time of my life. A student searching for meaning in life was finally able to get a direction, thanks to the people I was able to meet and talk to in Uttar Pradesh. Some of them truly opened up about their lives to me. I found a way to make my education meaningful by connecting to the grassroots through this internship.

This was the first of its kind in India[1] and I was determined to get the required permission from my dean. Accordingly, I pushed around all of the massive paper work and this being the first in a government set-up, I managed to get permission to do exactly that. My three-month internship started in March 2009, and at about the same time, Lok Sabha elections were happening in India. I zeroed down on a newly formed regional party in Tamil Nadu led by an actor. My job was to find out the ways in which this regional party

[1] Pallavi Polanki. 'Join Politics, Young Man'. *Open*, 6 June 2009. https://openthemagazine.com/features/india/join-politics-young-man/

could be positioned better in south Tamil Nadu. With a new party and imperfect systems in place, I was thrown around on a day-to-day basis. But with the elections around, I was fully sucked into the everyday operations of running behind the candidates who might need any help. Typical of any political party that thrives on dynamism I was just doing whatever everybody wanted out of me. Though it was not an organised internship, it gave me a real opportunity to see campaigns, the running of ground-level operations, the marathon effort that goes into managing the whole election set-up and, most importantly, the power of vote in a democracy like ours. That stint also made me determined not to look at politics as a career in the near future as it was too messy and appeared as an unscalable wall to me. Back on campus post my internship and with a small seed planted in my head by all this running around, I decided to give a serious look at the Indian Civil Services. I felt this was the best option for me at that time, given that I had ruled out being in the forefront of Indian politics after that experience.

The Preparation Days

The first thing that comes to one's mind when somebody aspires to take the exam is the large volume of syllabus they have to cover and the somewhat opaque examination process. Frankly, I didn't know a thing about this at that point of time. I didn't see this examination process as insurmountable. I took a train to Delhi on a weekend, found out the famous coaching institutes available through the internet and decided to do a recce of those. I decided to go to the first institute on my list and was hoping that I would be able to find a like-minded student there who would be in a position to guide me. As fate would have it, I was able to find one Dr Mahesh in my first shot at that first coaching institute. He was a doctor from Chennai who had decided to take a career break and prepare for the Civil Services by staying in Delhi. A kind hearted person, he was pretty amazed by my audacity to think what I was thinking—to take a train and walk in just like that. He took me to his place of stay and was kind enough to teach me the basics of the exams over the next few hours. He also promised to share with me all of the study material he was using. In the world of mindless competition, this was immensely kind and if I have to owe anybody for the privilege of entering the civil service and serving our public, it would be him. Just like that, my preparation started on a whim. Every month, once or twice,

I managed to find time to shuttle between Delhi and Lucknow to collect materials and to pick on his brains. Studies were becoming equally tough in IIM as well with the workload piling up. One thing most students of IIM will agree on is that getting into an IIM looks like an easy task after a point of time and you start focusing desperately on finding a way to get out. Day by day, that starts to look tougher and tougher with the syllabus and classes.

With friends there sharing the bulk of my load for internal projects and assignments, I was able to free up some time for preparation. Living between Lucknow's winter and its scorching summer, my only purpose was to wriggle out four hours every day for civil service preparation. Fortunately, I was able to do that and crack my prelims. Then serious preparation started for my mains. When the dates of the UPSC Mains were announced, I could find at least three papers clashing with my trimester exams for MBA. Since postponing dates of the exam were out of the way, I had to convince my Student Union chairman and the dean to give me a special privilege. What we finally worked out was almost suicidal for me. I agreed to write the Mains exams in the morning and in the evening, I would write my regular MBA exam. One day, when I had two Mains exams in the morning and afternoon, I had to take one of my regular exams late in the evening. I don't how I managed to do all of that. The lesson I learnt then, and one which I continue to believe in, is the power of the human mind to adapt to anything when push comes to shove. With all the hard work and jugglery, I was able to pull clear the UPSC Mains exam. At the same time, I graduated my MBA programme with an above-average mark as well.

The final hurdle of the whole Civil Services exam was the interview and this was scheduled exactly twenty days after my graduation. For those twenty days, I went to Delhi to focus on my interview preparations. Unfortunately, by then, my doctor friend decided not to continue with his preparations anymore and proceeded to his hometown. I felt guilty as he walked more than half the way along with me to achieve the improbable. But I truly believe good people like him are always destined for better things. I finally gave my interview and returned home. Without a job, and not taking one consciously, I was quietly confident that I would get into the final selection. Finally, the results were out and I was slotted in the final list as well. With a rank hovering close to the mid-200s, I was eligible for the Indian Police Service (IPS) but I had filled up my application form with Indian Administrative Service (IAS) as my primary choice. Without a clue about the actual working of these services, I went mostly by what I had read in the media and what I had got from the circle of Civil Service preparation gang. I had no clue about policing, especially the IPS and kept it as option two. When I looked at my score card, I saw what I had expected to see—my written exam scores were patchy and were bordering on the average and what tilted the scale in my favour were my interview scores. Out of 300, I had managed to score 240. Getting eighty per cent in the interview was almost close to impossible; only a couple of aspirants managed to get it in an examination year. Perhaps my life's experience till then helped me in my interview and the board was able to see through that. Most of my answers revolved around common sense and I felt they were more grounded. There are times in our lives when we can feel our whole life coming together. Deeds that appeared meaningless at the moment of doing them appeared totally meaningful for me when I was sitting in front of complete strangers, answering their questions. When the board was testing me on reforms needed in the Indian agricultural sector, I was absolutely there, and likewise for rural development. Not being text-book-driven has its values when we dig deep to find answers that resonate with us and for which we can take complete ownership. This was a quality that I could identify with and always played on it. Feeling neither elated nor dejected, I decided to give the exam again before I was to join the training at the National Police Academy (NPA), Hyderabad. With the time gap available, it was convenient for me to write the exam again before getting into the grueling police training academy. It was now time to leave for Hyderabad and begin a new chapter of my life.

Training Days at NPA and LBSNAA

The National Police Academy (NPA), named after one of India's most illustrious sons and its iron man, Sardar Vallabhbhai Patel, is located in Hyderabad. Spread over a sprawling 300 acres, it is at once an imposing and venerable institution. When I walked through its hallowed gates for the first time, I could feel the sense of a new beginning right then. The guards with their strict demeanour signalled on the end of our playfulness and naivete. This two-year-long training period was such, that it would scare even bravehearts. The newness of the policing culture, built on discipline and hierarchy was not something one could quickly get used to. Most of the probationers—as we were called—who come to this venerable institution hail from various parts of India and with unique backgrounds. That is the greatest strength of the Indian Civil Services selection. I have not seen two similar individuals in the past ten years in my service. Each person had walked a unique path to arrive where he was. For every aspirant hoping to join the Civil Services, he can see one of his own inside the system who must have come exactly the same way as the aspirant, thereby igniting in him a hope and a belief.

Some of the probationers humbled you. They endured some of the worst that life can throw at a person and still, here they were. With our crew haircuts to the clockwork precision maintained across indoor and the outdoor training, one was keenly made aware of the fact that this training was not to be taken lightly. The trainers, who are fondly called *ustads* by the generations of officers trained before us, were the keepers of tradition and didn't leave anything to chance with their training. The laggards were pulled out and polished till they improved, our attitude was noted closely and usually, slowly but steadily, trainees were sculpted into officers. Like many of my batchmates, I had also entered into the system without any clue about policing. Little did we know that we were changing from the inside. We did not feel this but most of our close family members and friends noticed with startled looks. The morning runs, combined with the rigorous physical training, were making us fit. Our uniforms arrived within a month of joining and one could see the starry-eyed men and women who had walked through those gates a while back, getting ready to shoulder the responsibilities of the nation. The probationers are exposed to, among other things, horse riding, rock climbing, shooting (weapon handling), swimming and the much-hated drill. As if these weren't enough, we were taken across the country for specific attachments with specialised units. Most of us had entered as individuals with a sense of achievement and prestige but the training, by its very design, had found a way to break us open and make us humbler.

No doubt NPA kept most of us busy, but we enjoyed being busy bees. The indoor classes passed in a blur as most of the probationers were too tired to know what was happening inside the classroom after our hectic morning outdoor sessions. In the middle of training some of us got our results and destiny made sure I was selected into IPS again—while the first time around Iwas chosen into a cadre allotment in Uttarkhand, this time, it was in a different cadre allotment in Karnataka. By this time, the love for khaki was so overpowering, I chose to stay the course and opted for Karnataka, keeping in mind my wife's career prospects as she was working for a private organisation.

I had very fond memories of my training. Heading the social service club of the academy, the Samvedi Society, was a highlight. This kept me busy on the weekends as I had to conduct an Alcoholics Anonymous (AA) programme to de-addict some of our lower level staff who were addicted to alcohol. I was also parallelly in-charge of a special needs school and an *anganvadi* school run especially for the children of our staff members. These two regular activities and other occasional activities of the club kept me really busy apart from our daily schedule. I also found my latent talent for debate coming out in the academy and normally I would be among top three in most of the events. In short, NPA made me who I am. It gave a voice to my hopes. Time spent with those special needs' children healed me from the inside of my own insecurities. I used to forcibly bring the staff to the AA programme and sit along with them and hear them speak. When they narrated how they got into a life revolving around alcohol, I could see the exact tipping points in their lives and how they slipped. It was humbling when any staff member came out of the addiction and thanked me when they become sober. Even though I may not have personally helped in their recovery, spending time with them on Sundays seemed worth it, especially because it seemed, as if, to their families, what I was doing made a difference. They were not shouting at the wife and children anymore and most importantly, they seemed to have more self-respect. It was a massive privilege being able to do this as people willingly let me into their lives and I enjoyed every moment of this work.

Without a doubt, every single officer who had passed out of the NPA would say that he or she enjoyed the outdoor periods more. These outdoor sessions were conducted according to the squads to which we are allocated. The squad loyalty was so strong that people maintained squad-level connections right up to retirement and even after that. The NPA training had to be very different from other trainings because they had to break us and recreate us so that we became capable of shouldering the burdens of leadership. As officers in the field, with thousands of people watching us, there's always great emphasis on creating that 'officer-like quality' in us. Many may not have possessed these qualities when they entered through the academy gates, but the training made sure that we not only became brave officers, but also respectable gentlemen with an unshakable sense of honour and duty. These are very important qualities for a police officer and displaying them will not bring us greatness, failing to adhere to them will most certainly bring us great shame. Most importantly, however, the course of justice is compromised if these qualities are not ingrained in officers. The way I see it, every single quality is moulded and imbibed into us in the playgrounds when we play our team games like hockey, football, cricket and throwball. Most of us were not fully moulded into a group that puts our self interests aside and many of us were still in that ultra-competitive zone as individuals. All of these games which require togetherness more than anything else made us bond and some of my batchmates, eventually, were willing to do anything for the squad that we belonged to. The same was drilled into us in every single outdoor session like rock climbing, swimming, horse riding, drill sessions and especially when shooting bullets on a target. Some of these events required precise coordination and total trust on our fellow participant. These real bullets can kill anybody if a gun is mistakenly tilted at even a couple of degrees as there are batchmates, trainers and staff members standing all around us. We are taught to be in sync with each other and with our weapons, not even a single incident has happened in NPA's history. This is a testament to the group dynamics and the high level of awareness that NPA is quickly able to build into each of us.

We were also lucky in training as we had a visionary director in the form of Mr VN Rai, a 1977 batch officer from Haryana cadre. He was determined to change the training with his holistic methodology that had the core of humanness built into it. The motto of the batch, 'Sensitive Police for an Empowered Society' accurately reflected what the batch set out to achieve. The IPS training was increasingly becoming paramilitary-like in terms of brute-force and might. Rai was single-handedly responsible for fostering more care and the ethos required for civil policing. Many field visits were organised to enable us to confront the real world problems like in slums, deal with trafficked children and women, and to be more empathic towards the downtrodden. Often, they are the most neglected part of our policing and he rightly emphasised on it. In fact, all of the activities that we indulged in the Samvedi Society, the social service arm of NPA, were planned and supported by him. Our batch, 64 RR, in my opinion, has been very different in on-field performances over the last decade and the credit should go entirely to him for being courageous enough to lead that change.

Two things stood out for me in training—our horse-riding sessions and the bungee jump that some of us did at Rishikesh. Nobody in the academy was able to give me a convincing reason as to why horse riding was introduced in the IPS training. One theory that was floated around was that once we are able to control the horses, we will be in a position to control humans. I always felt it was the opposite. Handling horses is tougher than handling some of the choicest criminals in the real world, if i can slip in a joke. Horses in the NPA were never in a mood to listen to anybody and they operated on their own rhythm. Only a fool would think that he could control one of those horses. Whenever anybody tried, they would get booted by the horse. The intelligent probationers allow the horses to control them and so safely managed to pass the much-feared horse-riding exams. For me, riding a horse gave me a sense of freedom and a quiet confidence that enabled me to handle the problems that crop in life. When some of us (eight, to be precise) were selected for the Tonk Cup, a competition to decide who is the best rider of the batch, the training process that we had to undergo gave me a new understanding about this animal. We had to do some impossible jumps in show jumping and also had to exhibit a fine degree of control over the horses in the dressage event. The finesse with which the horses can operate when handled the right way and the extent to which the horses were willing to get pushed taught me the fine line between risk and recklessness. The lessons learnt by sitting on that majestic animal still remain dear to me after almost a decade. The final answer to why the horseriding classes in the NPA are continuing is still a mystery but my guess is this—because the horses are there and they have to be used. These animals, almost numbering close to eighty, who have support staff assigned to them, can't be disposed of.

One important life-altering moment that occurred for me was when we were made to go bungee jumping at Rishikesh as part of our course. This jump, located at one of the tallest points of India (vertical drop of 330 metres) seemed to be very doable when we were briefed. The terror started to strike when we neared the jumping board. The height disoriented most of us when we saw human beings looking like small ants below. Finally, with our ego and prestige at stake, as all the batchmates were watching each other to see who chickened out, there was no choice; we had to jump. Once off the board, it was pure exhilaration—we felt like birds flying without any care in the world. I learned a very important lesson about risk that day. I was afraid to jump in the first instance because of the fear of death. That was the single biggest obstacle—the fear of the unknown—that I realised didn't allow us to truly be ourselves. This fear had always lingered in my mind as a silent voice telling me many things: this was dangerous and shouldn't be done; somebody couldn't do this previously; you better be careful. This wasn't allowing me to give my best as I was focussing only on the results. But that one bungee jump changed my perspective about the fear of the unknown. I started to perceive risks very differently the moment I landed after my jump and as a very different person. Many people ask me, can one jump make this shift happen? I only tell them to try it and experience it for themselves. Risk is always perceived differently by different people. For somebody jumping three metre into a pool will be a risk. For some, allowing their loved ones to cross the road all alone is a risk. For an Indian army soldier, it could be standing at the Siachen border in -40°C, watching the enemy 30 metres away, not knowing when the bullets will whizz by is a risk. But that bungee jumping moment helped me perceive risks differently; I started to look at risks with respect to the planning and precautions one could take before going ahead and doing what till then seemed near impossible. With three levels of safety harnesses tied to our bodies, even if one or two failed, there was still the last one clinging to our bodies. That operator too had a spotless record when it came to fatal accidents. Why then, I thought, should I worry, given I have already taken precautions? This shift for me was very important as like most of you, when I planned for anything that I considered risky, I always double checked the planning and precautions so that none of our men were put in the harm's way.

The Lal Bahadur Shastri National Academy of Administration (LBSNAA) located in the beautiful Mussoorie, Uttarkhand, is where the combined training of IAS, IPS and IFS is conducted. Initially, all of the All India and Group A Services used to be together and due to the paucity of space, it's been restricted to three services now. I came to it a bit later than most as the norm is to undergo this training before the commencement of IAS, IPS or IFS's individual training. This short ninety-day programme is called the Foundation Course (FC) and is designed to build batch camaraderie and help us understand the Indian Civil Services. Over the years, this training has become very hectic as each subsequent batch has only new courses added to it without the deletion of any of the old courses.

I enjoyed my FC course as I had the opportunity to do some interesting things there. I also contested my first elections there by standing for the post of the Secretary of Management Circle (a club) and won. It's always an exciting feeling when we are forced to stand before our batchmates and offer our pitch to them explaining why we are the best candidate for the job. Competing pitches from batchmates made the the whole process all the more exciting. What did they think of my pitch? Did they like it? Did the other guy charm them better? Is there anything else at play here apart from all the strings that each of us already pulled? In the end, the real question is, did I influence the influencers of the group? It was ultimately a way to know if people really accepted you. Finally, when the results were declared and when I knew I'd won my first election, the responsibility of that job hit me immediately. I guess this is what most elections are about. This moment also invariably stayed with me for a long time as my faith in myself was tested. A month later, I had to stand for one more election for the post of chairman to conduct the India Day celebrations.

India Day is a very important event in LBSNAA. Probationers from all states get to showcase their state's uniqueness by performing its dance forms and presenting their cuisine for others to savour. For me, that whole month went in coordinating all of these for different states, be it inviting their chefs, artists and other notable personalities. Obviously, my classroom learning took a back seat but I didn't bother much as I was confident that I could make it up in the final exams. LBSNAA also gives the opportunity to undertake one difficult trek when the course is about to culminate. I chose to trek to the Roopkund Lake out of the options given to us as it seemed to be the hardest. This trek turned out to be the defining moment of my stay in Uttarakhand. The overall seven days of trek taught me very valuable lessons about life. The sense of accomplishment lay not in reaching the destination alone but being able to pull anybody along who started to feel it wasn't for them. The final two days of that brutal climb in the cold made couple of our trekmates literally give up but we pushed them (and sometimes pulled them) to complete that climb to Roopkund Lake. The exhilaration of making the team complete the task as a whole unit is something to be felt. This trek generated in me a lifelong passion for the Himalayas and over the years, I have returned to explore parts of this majestic mountain range.

I was humbled when on FC's graduation day, I was chosen to receive 'Sangay Lhaden Shenga-Esprit de Corps' and '1968 Batch Silver Jubilee Esprit de Corps Gold Medal'. Both of these awards are normally awarded to the probationer who has shown exemplary leadership during this combined training. Unlike other awards, this is voted on by the probationers themselves on a secret ballot. Though there is nothing great in winning or losing a medal, when some of India's best think I'm doing something right, it only gives an additional bit of energy and motivation to be on that path. The sense of camaraderie that was built in those ninety days would remain with us through our lifetimes. We could subsequently see this in our professional lives as for us any official help needed across India was purely dependent on making a single phone call. Any one of our batchmates would be posted in any part of our country and they would move heaven and earth to get the job done. We were able to get a lot of critical work done only by the power of the friendship that was forged here and not by any titles after our names.

Our total training—LBSNAA as a foundation course and NPA where the policing ropes are learned—culminates in a regal passing out parade in NPA, Hyderabad in front of enthusiastic family members and friends. This signalled that all of our hard work, in the blazing Hyderabad heat, with our companions who had become our lifelong friends, was over. After the passing out parade, we had our All India Darshan, which meant visiting different parts of the country depending on the zones we were allotted, to see the important landmarks and places of national importance. Immediately after this, we were sent back to our respective states for practical training in the state's affairs and later called back to the NPA for a three month Phase-II programme. When all of these were over, we earned the right to call ourselves as 'officers'. After two gruelling years of training, exposure and experience of life, we were no longer just probationers.

Stepping into Khaki

After my training at the NPA, I was sent back to my cadre in Karnataka. After a short wait, all five of my batchmates and I got our postings as Assistant Superintendent of Police. I was to be posted in Karkala. Karkala is located in Udupi district, amidst the beautiful Western Ghats and has its own rich history. An active Jain centre earlier and now a thriving cashew hub of India, the police sub-division there was quite run-of-the-mill as far as police sub-divisions go. A quiet and compact division with seven police stations with a myriad of challenges but nothing extraordinary. It was also the hub of Karnataka's left-wing extremism which is now on a decline. Added to that, there were the routine law and order challenges like the simple dispute between a Hindu and a Muslim that invariably took a communal turn once the leaders jumped in to solve the issue, regular crimes, traffic-related offences including road traffic accidents and suicidal deaths. Apart from these, we had a lot of regulatory work like checking the violation of any government-established rules and procedures which took precedence in a state that was conscious of its revenue generation like a bar being open beyond its stipulated time or a quarry mined illegally.

I still remember my early days in Karkala. In the first few weeks, I didn't have a clue of what was left and right. Officers would brief me as if I knew everything.

Not knowing the Kannada language and in an absolutely alien police culture, issues of whom to trust and differentiating between a friend and a foe were the initial set of challenges. Added to this was the inevitable 'call on's', where we met all the officers from the other departments in an informal way. This was mainly to get to know them and also to show my face as a new government functionary in the district. Many of the age-old customs were to be followed, like meeting most of my police seniors in Bangalore. The most exciting part of this was getting to listen to the stories of their policing experiences, some of which happened over thirty years back. Though most of them might not be relevant today, the practical wisdom that we gleaned from them was priceless.

When we settled down and got into a routine, the job of a police officer hit us like a truck when going at a full speed as we saw the workings of the government at a very close level. The responsibilities overwhelmed us when we started meeting the public and got into the groove of solving their problems. Anytime a new officer took charge, we could see people bringing their old problems with a renewed confidence, some of which were even three decades old, and literally expected miracles from us. The kind of confidence people have in this steel frame of a system and their belief that their problems will get solved by the invisible government and the visible government machinery has to be seen to be believed.

In the initial days of my Assistant Superintendent of Police tenure, most of the time, when any person spoke to me in the privacy of my office, I would listen with incredulity. Some of their stories and life experiences were out of the world to me. For a civilian till now and to be an officer suddenly, to whom people bare their hearts, came as a rude awakening. I was convincing myself initially that because of being a police officer, only people with problems naturally approach me. I was also really dismayed by some of the horrendous acts human beings are capable of, the unspeakable cruelty that exists in some marriages and the depth of sorrows people go through when they lose their loved ones. Those were very tough and many times I carried these stories home, to the dinner table as well. At the same time there were also a few moments of bliss, seeing the goodness that some human beings exhibit. I have seen people braving their lives jumping into a river and rescuing a child or entering into a building that is on fire to rescue an old woman. I have also seen a few brave feats like the villagers in the rural areas of Karkala rescuing a trapped leopard from a village well. They were doing this without a care for their safety and were only worried for the traumatised animal. Most of these heroes didn't wait for a government representative to come and their actions were very simple and pure. They just did what they felt was right and that was it. I used to be amazed by some of these people. I have seen all of these acts in Indian movies but to see them in real life was different. The joy of wiping a tear from a common man's life invariably made up for the lows that we went through in our daily jobs, like seeing a young man die in an accident, a suicide or a murder.

The emotions that I went through—as many other policemen also go through—can only be termed as a rollercoaster ride. It depends on the order of the people who enter our offices on a particular day. The first person who entered might have lost a loved one to a suicide or a road traffic accident and would have come for some procedural formality and the second person would come with the story of domestic violence and abuse. Like this, each person who entered the office had a story to tell and an experience to share. This roller coaster of emotions that we went through taught us many invaluable lessons and helped us see our society with a depth that we otherwise might not have.

Within a few months of settling down, I started to see my job for what it was. With patience, when I started to survey things around me, I could see that society was not as calm as it seemed from the outside. It was, and continues to be, very turbulent if we look a few levels below the surface. The rich have problems, the poor have them too and all the so-called VIPs have it in abundance. I could see that many of the problems were self-created. Without a proper application of the mind, attempting to solve any issue, makes the knot harder and the harder the knot is, the tougher it becomes for us to unknot it.

When I was reviewing the case files to know what was happening to get a first-hand account of things, I was shocked by the data staring at me. I'm presenting to you some of which I recall. A murder case was registered and the accused arrested because he chose to hit his victim with a crowbar in a fit of anger as the victim diverted the water flow from a side canal to his farm. I thought it could be one man's rage and might not be common. I was surprised to see that eighty per cent of murders were committed in a fit of rage (the better phrase would be 'in a moment of insanity'). When I reviewed the accident files and tried to learn from our officers, the results were pretty staggering. Most people, I found, died in road accidents for one reason, if I can use the official terminology—driving in a rash and negligent manner. This could be over speeding, not using a helmet, dangerous overtaking and so on. It was pretty striking. We were trained in one of the premier institutes of India to investigate crimes and hunt down the culprits. If the culprits turned out to be our own minds what do we do? There was no clear-cut answer for that. That's when clarity struck me. This job was not about machoism, bashing up the bad guys and flying from one building to another. Most police institutions are designed with fear and respect built into our positions, our offices and right down to our rooms. Even our uniforms with stars and medals and the tough looking belt that we wear don't look normal. If you expect us to run with our uniforms on to catch a bad guy, chances are, we might not even start with that paraphernalia on.

The photographs that hang in our offices, of previous police chiefs and other important police officers, in some districts dating back all the way to the British times, looks very different to present-day officers. With big handlebar moustaches and puffed up chests, the toughness they exhibited was needed for a different time. Those times, a few decades back, were different. Police responsibilities were different. I was very clear by then that our current roles, in a decade or so, would have become very different and would demand our empathy and patient listening. More than flying in the air and fighting, we had to become healers. This was an important understanding for me as I felt it would guide me on a clear path and motivate my colleagues to be on a similar wavelength as mine.

The Time for Selling My Vision

It's easy to sell a vision to police men and women who work under us in our initial years. Like the public, they also look at us with a hope for change. It's not that officers before us were bad and we are the only great people sitting in our seats. All officers before us did their best and the current young breed are leading by example as well. The hope a policeman has of a young officer is very simple. It revolves around their dignity and they way they are treated. Many a times, we fail to treat policemen as human beings. Them doing an uncommon job doesn't mean we have to treat them uncommonly. I always believed and continue to believe, the role performed by our lower ranking policemen—Police Constables (PC), Head Constables (HC) and Assistant Sub-Inspectors (ASI)—who make up close to ninety per cent of our force is unnatural. They work on average for about fourteen hours a day on the job. If we include their commuting time as well, it might easily jump to two-thirds of their waking life. On top of that, they don't get day-offs and it will not be a surprise to learn that they may have missed all their dear ones' important moments, major festivals and so on. They work continuously and over a point of time, their entire life gets engulfed by work. They tend to lose sensitivity and begin to view every situation as a problem that can be solved by hitting it with a hammer. All of this for what? Their pay is a pittance and they get paid one of the lowest government salaries. On top of it, they don't get respect within the station as well. The police hierarchy will sit over each rank—an ASI will transfer his anger and helplessness on an HC and the HC on a PC. The PC, in turn, lashes out on you and me—the general public.

I was very motivated to help my officers and men to see this. As Albert Einstein had brilliantly said, 'A fool is somebody who does the same thing again and again but expects a different result every time'. This is one of my favourite quotes and I used to repeat this ad nauseum to my men. Once I was able to convince my officers—Deputy Superintendent of Police (DySP/DSP), Circle Inspectors (CI) and Sub-Inspectors (SI)—we got to the tough job of convincing our men to take a hard look at all our habits and to find a new path to get things done. We decided on the following action points as a team and to put this into action straight away:

1. Everybody up to the ranks of ASIs needed to take a weekly off and not show up in office. Though this provision was made in Karnataka by one of our able former Chief of Police, Shri Ajay Kumar Singh, it was hardly put in action. Most often, *bandobusts* or VIP movements keep cropping up at the last minute to pour water over all their well-laid plans of a weekly holiday. After a point of time, the officers stopped granting this as there was something or the other that kept the station busy. Weekly off meant roughly fourteen per cent (1/7th) of the force need

to be on off-duty daily. Adding to it were the daily leaves; we were prepared for twenty per cent of the force not being available on any particular day.

2. Empowering the lower ranks to decide for themselves when they want to take their leaves. We encouraged the lower ranks of men to decide in advance and let us know when they needed their fifteen days of block annual leaves. I encouraged them to take a minimum of twenty days of Earned Leave (EL) every year apart from their fifteen days of Causal Leave (CL). All of their leaves, by accounting for the overlapping of dates within the station, were sanctioned at one go. By empowering them with certainty of their leaves, I have seen miracles happen.
3. Refinement of language was brought in. This is another important observation I had, that officers and men weren't using a proper or a refined kind of communication amongst themselves. When the standard of communication goes down inside a police station, no wonder it reflects on the communication we have with the public. Senior officers were gently advised initially and reprimanded later when they were found to be using abusive language with their juniors and the same standards were applied at all levels.
4. Importantly, we tried to build a picture that they are not alone doing some unimportant work. Like the story of a mason saying that he is building a beautiful cathedral and not some cement building, we did vision building workshops for them. We helped them to understand the importance of their job and their role in nation building.

5. No pressure was to be passed downwards, starting from me. One of the basic problems with police hierarchy is that we tend to panic too easily. When something goes wrong, barring very few leaders, the buck is always passed downwards. In a law and order setting with fast-emerging scenarios, the officers have to be quick on their feet and show courage. It's also a possibility that a few times they might not do a good job despite their trying. As long as it's not by deliberate design but a failure to correctly judge the situation, I made it a point to encourage them to act. For me, failing to act is unacceptable when compared to acting and making a few mistakes on the way.

These are all easy to talk about in workshops or in group settings. But the core group of some of my officers and I were really determined to get this done. So we decided to put in systems and processes to make sure all of these were consciously followed. That's how we got four out of seven police stations ISO 9001:2000 certified in the year 2013–14 for process control. We came up with a system where not only the weekly day-offs were built in but also, for the sake of efficiency, the time taken to process a complaint from start to finish was put in. Though we were one of the first to get so many stations certified together, I was very clear about the fact that without the officers buying into this idea, all of these would die a slow death. So I encouraged officers to lead from the front, take ownership of whatever they were doing and consequently take credit that came with it as it rightfully belonged to them. My job, I felt, with all the unimaginable powers my office held, was to act as a shield around my men and officers and guide them, when required, to always take that correct path.

After a point of time, I could see small, incremental changes at the police-station level. To respect people who work for us, I refused to take an orderly as an Assistant Superintendent of Police. I also didn't want to stay in my designated quarters (which was right behind my office), as men and officers would invariably congregate around me and their family members might be forced to take care of my family members, even if only as a goodwill measure. I shifted to a private accommodation with only my wife for company. My officers used to see me buying groceries, walking around the town in my t-shirt and civvies (civilian clothes) and going to a gym or to the movie hall, all by myself. This, I felt, was very important for me as I didn't want to live in the ivory tower, sit there and start advising. I started to clearly separate my professional life from my personal life. I led by taking that much-needed break for myself on a Sunday and encouraged my officers to do so. In short, I wanted them to be normal and human.

Challenges to the Vision Plan

When I reviewed weekly off days after a month, I found some people had worked all thirty days non-stop. Not only was it making me angry, but it was also demotivating to say the least. Slowly I started calling them to my office to get a first-hand account of why they wanted to be workaholics. Some of the reasons I got from them truly reinforced a very strong lesson in me—of keeping our eyes open but ears on the ground. I asked my men a simple question: Who in the world would refuse to take a break? Their answers were stunning. One gave me the answer that if he didn't take the designated weekly off, the government paid him ₹350 for each of those days and in a month that amounted to saving ₹1400. Another told me that his family didn't want him at home and he would end up picking a fight with his wife if he is around. Yet another person said he didn't know what a holiday looked like. For about five years, he was functioning without a single day of leave.

Would anybody believe that? I realised they had almost become automatons. Not only had the job taken a lot out of them in the name of serving others, but it had also left them broken. They had become the final arbiters of many things that have broken in our system, even though, strictly speaking, it wasn't theirs to fix. This is only because they are overloaded with work, sometimes even the stupid ones and they have lost their ability to differentiate between critical, important and unimportant. I would like to elaborate on this before I delve into how we tried fixing these issues as well.

I have seen at my level and certainly at the police station level that we are expected to do anything and everything for the public. The calls to the station would ask the officers and men to fix light poles, clogged drains and in some cases, even do something about dead dogs that have not been taken away. Most of the times, our beat constables (the lowest denominator of a police station area is called beat and a constable is normally made in charge of that) carry all sorts of contact numbers with them. Among those in their contacts list are the person in charge of electrical matters, the local snake catchers, the Panchayat Development Officer (PDO) and the sanitation worker. A beat constable was actually performing the role of a superman, solving anything and everything. Even if he couldn't solve the problem, he was at least making a genuine attempt to.

During my initial interactions with the beat constables, I asked them why they carried around all these numbers. A senior constable stood up and said, 'Sir, if power goes out and doesn't come on time, there is always a possibility of chain snatching (this is a crime where usually a bike-rider very expertly plucks a chain, invariably a *mangal sutra*, from a lady's neck. Usually, the hapless lady would be walking down the road and would be in the wrong place and at the wrong time) taking place. Sometimes we have to check whether the fuse is gone because of lightning. If we don't check, we remain under the assumption that there is a power cut. So I need to have the electrical guy's number so that he can check the fuse. Bad roads and unrepaired potholes are a major cause for accidents in rural areas and in many places people have lost their lives just trying to evade a pothole. So, I'm in touch with the PDO to get it repaired immediately and this problem mostly occurs after the rainy season. There is also the problem of snakes entering into rural homes during the monsoon and people invariably call us. Sanitation workers are very much needed to clean up the dogs that are dying on the roads. For me every one of these numbers is important.'

I didn't know what to say. On one hand, I was over the moon to see how our men had big picture orientation that we intended to cultivate, how they were able to connect the issues around them and the crimes that happened in a society. On the other hand, I was equally frustrated as I just couldn't see a way out of this. How could we avoid overburdening our police personnel with the work of other people and departments? In a complex society like India, state power is exerted through a policeman. He is invariably seen as the state in motion. This is becoming a big headache with most departments not hiring because of the financial conditions of the respective state governments. Most branches of the government are run using contract workers. Some of our essential services like electricity, water, sewage and waste disposal are heavily dependent on contract owners. This lack of ownership percolates to other areas and very soon, the burden falls on policemen's heads.

Another reason why the vision fell apart was because of people's mindset. This started with the officers' lack of courage, especially the senior ones. For any small issue, men would be poured out into that area to take charge of whatever the matter at hand was. This happened, and continues to happen, from a temple festival to an important law and order incident. Every year, we only keep adding manpower to routine events. If there are ten men needed for a job, we make it a point to deploy fifteen there. This, I felt, was happening because nobody wanted to take total responsibility or have their 'skin in the game'. If at all anything were to go wrong, we could always say that we had added more manpower than the previous year and so could not be held accountable. This total misuse of the trust that a policeman place in their commanding officer eventually adds to their already-existing burden. If we add all of these together, we can understand the true burden that is placed on a policeman.

This led us to the second round of smaller reforms which included reducing manpower requirements for *bandobust* duties by building in checks and tougher approval processes for manpower deployment, encouraging family outings at the station level, helping our beat constables segregate core and non-core work and rigorously implementing all our vision plans without any deviation. As they say, anything in life is always a work in progress and we were prepared to wait for the changes to percolate in.

In the years in policing, I was also exposed to a much bigger war out there. Winning that war, which was a series of smaller battles, would be painstaking and time-consuming. But with experience, I was able to see the battles very clearly and make an attempt to learn from them. Perhaps my biggest take from the whole experience is the understanding that we never win anything permanently. Victory was only achieved by fighting the battles whenever they reared their heads.

CONFRONTING THE BATTLES

The daily long, hard and drawn-out ones

Understanding the Power of Perception

We all understand the power of perceptions and how it makes or breaks us. Nowhere does this play a more major role than in daily policing. The public looks at the police as an institution and has certain preconceived notions about the force itself. They expect a man in khaki to be daring, helpful, compassionate and most importantly, a problem solver. They also expect policemen to be fit. Perceptions, if found helpful, can be consciously cultivated to take the goodwill further. For instance, we can bring in a culture of fitness by encouraging and rewarding people who are fit or encourage the development of processes and systems to make policemen more compassionate and efficient. In some cases, negative perceptions or stereotypes, take policemen further away from the people to whom they are accountable and for whom they are responsible.

During my initial visits to colleges, one of my favourite questions to my student audience was, 'How many of you think our policemen are corrupt?' A sizeable number of hands would go up. I followed it up with another question, 'How many of you have personally paid a bribe to a person in uniform?' The enthusiasm of the audience ebbed and barely one-tenth of the hands that initially went up stayed that way. In a country like India, with its myriad problems, policing is not understood and policemen even less so. Almost every school student wanted to be a cop but none of them wanted to wear that uniform when they grew up. Why did this turn-around happen? Was it because when growing up, we tend to lose our idealism? Or was it simply because policemen were made the beefy villains in movies? What would it take to overcome this perception? This story is an attempt to remove some myths and to be genuinely reflective on the life of a policeman.

Till about a decade back, I was amongst the people who believed every potbellied policeman was corrupt, making more than enough money to indulge in pleasures. I believed policemen were continual reminders of Englishmen who had left India. This is because most people tend to see a policeman as a colonial hangover. Post training at the NPA, as mentioned earlier, I was assigned to a district in Karnataka for practical training. Day one of my career taught me a lesson that remains unforgettable to this day.

When I landed in this allotted district, I was received by a driver in a neatly kept old jeep. As was customary, he made me sit in the front seat, locked my door and went to the driving seat. I could clearly see him struggling to fit into his seat as the seat belt was too tight. He easily weighed upwards of 110 kilogrammes. The beginning weeks of a probationer's time are slightly volatile and we become acutely aware of things which deviate from the 'norm', thanks to the twenty-four months of training. How long one maintains that before getting tainted is purely left to oneself. This is also the time that our conscience is close to the ideal and works with the mindset that anything in India can be changed and all social evils can be eradicated. I guess, my driver understood me too well as he must have received many probationers over the years.

At the first possible opportunity, I questioned why he was looking unfit. Did he not take pride in his uniform? He just smiled out of respect while I could clearly see how uncomfortable my question had made him. He said he would answer my question after a week. My first week just rolled by through a haze of calling-on rituals, office adjustments, getting amazed at the sheer volume of work, etc. This was also the week that I finally got the long-awaited opportunity of taking a closer look at the Indian constabulary and the fundamental shift that is taking place at the police station level. The traditional view in policing is to have a disciplined and unquestioningly loyal force but I could see social boundaries quickly dissolving as the new recruits were fully different from the older versions of khaki. They were more educated, in some cases even with a post-graduate degree, with a definite fire in their bellies and with an attitude of being equal to everybody in the police department despite the hierarchies within which we operate.

True to his word, my driver volunteered to answer, the week after. He opened up once he got a measure of me, I guess. This time he was more on my face with his reply.

'Sir, a young ASP like yourself must have observed that I pick you up by 9 AM. For that I leave my home by 7 AM, attend my daily roll call (it's at a central location where daily attendance is taken and duty for the day is allocated), reach the depot to collect the vehicle (normally in a police unit, the vehicles are parked in a central location), clean it up, which takes anywhere between forty-five minutes to an hour and drive down to your place, reaching fifteen minutes ahead of your scheduled time. I'm always with you wherever you go. When you go for lunch, unfortunately you take only a thirty-minute break which means, I get twenty minutes only as I have to be back ten minutes before you come. I can neither carry my lunch nor afford to eat outside in a good place. So, I go to the most economical hotel nearby to eat whatever they can give me for ₹40. In the evening, you invariably reach your home by 9 PM. By the time I go back, return the vehicle, complete the documentation (like mileage and trip sheet) for the day, it is usually 10:15 PM. I reach my home not before 10:45 PM. Now you understand why I am fat.'

I had no words. My perception of him was punctured in that moment. I'm sure many of you also have a perception about a certain thing, even a policeman. It was a good time for me to see very clearly how much of it was true. At the same time, I was also initiated into a world that was far away from textbook idealism; a world that needed a lot of listening and a lot less talking.

There is another incident I can distinctly recall in the first year of policing that equally left a deep impression on me. The Superintendent of Police (SP) of my district called me at the very end of my career as ASP (within a few days I was to be promoted as SP). He told me that I needed to rush to the nearest sub-division of the district and take charge of a communal issue. I immediately left for that area and based on local enquiries, with inputs from the police, I found out who the main culprit responsible for creating the trouble was. With a small team, I rushed to his home to pick him up for enquiry. When we reached there, we found out that he was yet to reach home from sea (he was a fisherman by profession and belonged the majority community of that area). We went and waited near the jetty, saw him alighting from his boat and promptly picked him up. We took him to the local police station and after we were certain that he was the culprit, promptly arrested him and sent him to court. The court later remanded and sent him to the jail.

We called for an intercommunity meeting at the police station and spoke to the leaders on the need to maintain peace. In a couple of hours, we could see that the heat was starting to dissipate and the area was slowly gaining a semblance of normalcy. With peace returning, I returned to my headquarters in the nearby sub-division. By 3 AM in the morning, the local police called me to inform that there was a massive protest being organised against me in that area from 6 AM onwards. The local political leaders had taken control and had convinced the fishermen to not venture out into the sea that day. The rumour they were spreading against me was that I had arrested an innocent who was observing religious rituals as part of his pilgrimage. The plan seemed to be to unite a particular community in the name of religion, call for a day-long hartal and try to make the police cower to them in submission. This was a dangerous sort of game that was played many a times subsequently throughout my policing career. I got ready on the day and reached the place before the hartal started. I was sitting at the police station monitoring what was happening. The crowd assembled slowly and by noon there was a huge crowd and they were itching for a fight. By the time the rally started, there were close to 8,000 people—literally the whole town—and they were all marching towards the police station seeking 'justice'.

By that time, the SP of the district had arrived and I was asked to stay put in the station lest I anger the crowd by venturing out. I stayed in the station, mutely watching all that was happening. The local community leaders arrived first and they started the negotiation with the SP. Their demands were—to take action against me, to release the culprit who was lodged in the prison and make me apologise to the accused. Naturally, the police officers were opposing these idiotic demands. By the time the crowds reached the station, the police, believing the leaders will take responsibility for controlling the crowds, allowed them close to the station premises. There was massive slogan-shouting against me and the choicest of abuses were reserved for my family members.

With some pressure from the crowd, the SP agreed to let the accused out on bail. When word was sent to me to come out and talk to the protestors in a 'gentle way', I flatly refused. By then some people in the crowd had started pelting stones at the police station itself and I was asked to go inside the storeroom to 'hide'. This avoidable situation had escalated purely because of thorough mismanagement by the senior officers. Not only had they failed their uniform, they had also thrown me and my career under the bus that day. With a section of the crowd coming behind the police station and pelting stones at the window, I was genuinely scared that a part of the crowd, who were already out of control, might barge into the police station. For a mob of 8,000 a force of 300 outside and thirty men inside the station was of no match. I took out my service pistol, cocked it and was waiting for them to come inside the storeroom.

Finally, a few hours later and with their energy dissipated, the crowds dispersed and slowly things began to return to normal. The crowds had proved their point by bringing the accused out of jail by forcing the police to submit a favourable bail report. Later, I was told a grand reception party was organised and a welcome given to the accused as well. I felt extremely disappointed and angry that day.

I went home, applied for a day's leave and rested. When I analysed the whole thing calmly, I realised there was a lesson for me to learn from this incident and I was determined to learn it well. The first thing I understood was that a political leader, especially a community leader, would tap into people's innermost fears. Here, the two identities of somebody being a fisherman and from a particular religious community were used as a prop to create a story around the accused going on a certain pilgrimage. To add more colour, the pilgrimage clothes the accused was wearing was shown to the crowd. By this an 'insult' factor was added to the whole affair. When spoken about first in groups of five and then in groups of hundreds, in no time became a deadly cocktail of emotion and religious fervour. Here, the truth stood no chance. I had become the villain in this story and the need to defeat me brought together the 'underdogs'. This is how most movie plots were made and many political careers were constructed. Once I deciphered this puzzle, the sense of anger slowly left my system and I waited for a payback opportunity on the instigators as well as the accused who was released that day. I didn't know whether my time for payback would really come as I was due for a promotion as SP and a transfer to another place was also in the cards.

A day before my promotion, the district minister called me to inform that he had requested the CM to promote and post me in the same district as SP. Normally, it doesn't work that way as overnight I would become senior to my erstwhile colleagues. Hence, the government generally avoided doing it. I told the minister that I was duty-bound to follow the government's wishes. The very next day, an order arrived promoting me to the position of SP and posting me to the same district as I was already in. It was a bit of a complicated time as the old SP had completed only six months' tenure there. I met him, explained the situation to him and offered my apologies for putting him in the spot. Gracefully, he handed over the charge to me and proceeded to his next place of posting.

Within a few days of me taking over, seventeen days to be precise, the same town saw another communal incident. Since the local community had already tasted our blood, they were more vociferous this time. The perception they had of the police force and of me in particular were like this: week-kneed, susceptible to blackmail and prone to one-upmanship. I was determined to beat them at their own game. When the situation was getting out of hand and warranted a show of force, the policemen were given a free hand to go after the troublemakers. When stones were pelted at a religious place, a massive police force was mobilised and put into action; the troublemakers were caned when they tried to damage public property. Later, we arrested close to seventy-four people from both the communities who were part of this orchestrated violence. This time, to teach them a lesson, a magisterial permission was obtained to transfer them to a much larger district prison 400 kilometres away.

Here, to beat a negative perception, a different, stronger perception of the police being tough and ruthless was brought upon. We built on this incident and kept up our image of toughness and ruthlessness to maintain peace in that area for quite some time.

My mantras for winning the battle against perception:

1. Understand our inherent biases first as these are often the basis on which perceptions are formed.
2. Put ourselves in others' shoes before making a judgment or taking an action.
3. Rethink how our actions will be perceived. This thinking has to be done right in the middle of any crisis. This is purely the leaders job as others might not have the 360 degree view.
4. Be conscious of perceptions at play when meeting someone for the first time or hearing them speak without seeing them. Bring out the element of fact combined with interpretation of that fact to hearsay. The truth is some how hidden inside this.
5. Give the benefit of doubt to the opposite person, when needed to, as they are possibly also acting on perception and with less facts. Try and have a genuine conversation by being the first to reach out by sacrificing your ego.
6. When in anger, think about the points 1–5 twice!

The Pernicious Culture of a Bribe

I vividly remember the first time somebody tried bribing me. This was in the third week of my policing career. There was this farmer waiting in my office. Since the office was small, there used to be people milling around near the gate. I distinctly remember that gentleman who was carrying a small cloth bag and waiting outside, continuously being overtaken by people who entered the office after him. I told my office people to bring him inside and when I made him sit, all his emotions burst out at one go. I quickly understood that his is a long-standing land issue. A retired army personnel, who happened to have the plot of land next to his farm, was encroaching on his one acre of land. This farmer, being powerless, couldn't do much and could only protest. Understandably, the mightier neighbour couldn't be touched. This gentleman had tried complaining to the local police station. The first time the sub-inspector had faithfully gone there and tried solving this land issue by calling for the local surveyor. Once the ex-service man understood that land measurements would start, he started writing petitions against our officer. This petition process is one ordeal that most government officers and there is no option but to go through. Since all of these enquiries take a lot of time, no officer in their right mind would take these 'petition masters' head on.

So the sub-inspector took the next best option (and also, in his case, the wiser one) of telling this old gentleman that he could not do any spot visits after the first one and since it was a revenue subject, the police would not be able to interfere any further. Tragically, this emboldened the ex-service man and his daily troubles started only to increase. With no choice left, he came to my office once he got to know some 'new' officer had come. After hearing this whole story and ignoring the 'wise counsel' of my office people, I decided to take the bait. I visited the spot and enquired both the parties. The next day, I personally made my sub-inspector bring the local surveyor along, got the land measured and gave the gentleman his land back by demarcating it. I visited again for the third consecutive day and helped this man to get the fencing done as well. It was the first case where I took the risk of playing around the law and solved the issue. It was also the first of many and I started to skirt along the edges of law frequently by throwing away the precedents and procedures, if I felt the person upheld the Dharma. As expected, the ex-service man filed several petitions against me on frivolous grounds such as not a perfectly worn uniform and the cap not perched atop my head perfectly. There were sixty-four petitions against me by him over the next few years! I always felt concerned for his troubled soul whenever I was alerted to a new one from him against me. After a while, since many petition masters were after me, I stopped counting and didn't care to see who was after me.

A few months later, that old gentleman came to my office again and I thought the matter might have cropped up again. I asked him whether all is good with him. He quietly opened his bag, took out a ₹500 note and placed on my table. He said, 'Thank you, this is all I can afford'.

That scene broke me for two reasons. One, for the image he carried about the institution of police and two, I was pained by the fact that he might have previously had to pay any bribe to anybody. I asked him to take his money back, and hiding my anger, asked him, 'Why and who told you to pay this?' Without blinking, he gave a frank and direct answer. His answer was both hilarious and food for thought to me. He mentioned that if anybody, especially a government official, does any good work for him, he pays for it just like he pays for electricity and the bus. Though they are also government-provided amenities, he still pays. I went on a long monologue to explain to him the difference between government services and utilities, fully knowing that this gentleman would not understand what I was speaking about. The whole experience of trying to solve his issue taught me many invaluable lessons. Though, I served as the SP of the same district subsequently, I didn't get an opportunity to meet him again. I'm sure wherever he is, he must be doing well.

This was the starting point of understanding the complex phenomenon of the bribe. Over the course of my policing career, I saw some ugly incidents involving bribe in our offices and I was forced to be ruthless with some of my erstwhile colleagues. In some other cases, I was dismayed to see bribes being taken by some of our important public offices as a matter of routine. Some of these offices interacted with common citizens for their everyday needs, such as issuance of certificates, land records, traffic challans, driving licences, etc. With the division of responsibilities among the different police departments, law and order ones would be powerless to deal with a bribe complaint. With most states creating institutions of their own, such as Lokayutha and Anti-corruption bureaus, the common man mostly looks at those for bringing in that much needed positive change.

I have seen people being bribed because of the power dynamics between the seeker and the giver. When the seeker is in a position to deliver something—either legally or by creatively stretching the laws, power of their office automatically comes into the transaction. Citizens in a country like ours historically have felt powerless because of excessive reverence for authorities and the system itself that is not at its optimal efficiency. In our normal dealings, corruption has become a way of life. With officers at the local level sometimes being posted through means that are suspect, the quality that one expects from an institution is only going down. In the police force, the culture of bribery starts right from the recruitment process. A decade back, recruitments were so rife with corruption that any sane person would think twice before applying for the job as a police constable. With the judiciary's intervention, capacity building and the use of technology, corruption has lessened to a large extent. I'm not sure whether the same level of confidence can be placed in recruitments for the middle and senior positions as skeletons keep tumbling out every few years about the murky processes being employed.

Some states across India are known culprits as they seemed to have developed a whole ecosystem that thrives on corrupt practices for recruitment into government roles. Some have also creatively invented systems of brokering marriages for a candidate and a part of the dowry money goes as bribe to the selection board. With the courts taking a harsh view of these malpractices, technology seems to be a great leveller between the influential and the not so influential ones with the whole process being videotaped and documented. Still, the points where humans interact with each other, like interviews, are still places that need a thorough overhaul so that good and honest candidates are not lost.

Bribery at the recruitment stage that is introduced to many officers is one that they continue to associate with throughout their career, till they retire. If we look at the policing world real time, bribe plays a very important role. It starts right from the time an officer enters into a new posting. Most of the police postings are graded into four categories—tough and income-generating; tough and non-income-generating; easy to work and income-generating; easy to work and non-income-generating. This classification is based on the economic potential of the area and the nature of the policing challenges. Areas that are economically backward also tend to have issues like Naxalism, and these can be classified as tough and non-income generating areas. By non-income-generating I mean that there is no economic potential in the area, unlike say, a highway hotel where a policeman can encourage illegality, a big factory where labour problems are expected or some commercial establishments like restaurants and shopping malls where a fixed charge is paid as '*mamool*' (bribe) to the local officers. These areas attract either the idealistic police officers or the thoroughly useless ones.

Tough and income-generating are some areas with caste and communal conflicts that keep the officers on their toes and also have got some income-generating sources. These attract officers who are practical, efficient and also generally good but sometimes with suspect intentions. These areas can be managed by idealistic officers as well but since they don't allow the spoils of their office to percolate down and therefore, will not be preferred by the ecosystem there (like the political set-up or some senior officers situated in the place). These idealistic officers will be brought in once in a while when there is a severe caste or communal flare up or some major law and order issue. They are brought in to set the system to order before quickly being shunted out once the job is done. These areas are generally managed by the efficient ones who keep the wheel in motion without disturbing the status quo too much.

Easy to work and income generating areas are 'settled areas' in policing parlance and most major cities and city HQ's fall under this classification. This is where the heaviest fight is and the officers fight like cats and dogs to get posted. Easy to work and non-income generating areas again see officers who are either idealistic or useless. These are the areas that see major improvements during the times of a good officer but remain stagnant otherwise. These areas generally tend to be rural and backward.

The reason I have given this in detail is to help the readers understand that bribe in policing, is systemic. One of the ugliest scenes that we see is the concept of the local ruling politicians deciding who gets posted to their district, starting from a sub-inspector right up to the SP. Needless to say, money plays a huge role in getting the post. All of the above mentioned factors govern the amount of money that is to be exchanged. Good, idealistic guys continue to be side-lined while resourceful ones keep moving up the ladder. Some states have formalised this arrangement and it is so thorough, that a word has been given to the letter that the political leader sends to the government requesting for an officer—'minute'. Curiously, the governments, meaning the senior officers and the bureaucrats, actually go by this letter when posting officers.

This becomes a critical issue as the top tier is compromised. With the present style of politics and government formation, the system is always held at ransom by a coterie of established politicians and money bags. Both of these groups need officers of their choice at sensitive posts to protect their ill-gotten wealth. These officers establish a symbiotic relationship with these politicians and the careers of both the parties are aligned. With many politicians owning media houses both print and electronic—the required media coverage is given to the officer to promote him as an efficient and virtuous being. Unless this chain is broken, expecting systemic changes will remain a pipe dream. There are some who defend a bribe as something that is much required for a system to run, and for many of our citizens any bribe is bad and always an act of fleecing. Without systemic changes it's impossible to go after petty corruption and bribes of this above kind.

I had a very peculiar relationship with officers with respect to their efficiency and integrity. For me, I could count with my fingers the officers who were daredevils at work and had a great amount of integrity. They belong to the first category and a very miniscule one. The second category comprised of the efficient and the status quo-ist ones. The third were the totally useless and corrupt and the fourth group is pessimistic, useless and non-corrupt. In the initial part of my career, I used to be very harsh on all the categories of individuals except the first ones. Then I realised I'm creating two issues—one, I'm making the good guys the target for all the others' slander and political targeting and two, the other three categories of officers deliberately blocking the system from working. My efforts to transfer and bring good guys in were met with a laugh as I couldn't find enough good guys to bring in. Many idealistic and good people lost out in the initial part of their careers as they couldn't survive this ecosystem. I will not forget some of the efficient, most hardworking and non-corrupt officers for their work with me. They braved everything for me with even the system going against them sometimes. They gave their heart and went beyond their call of duty to right the wrongs, and in the process, suffered immeasurably. I'll salute them till my last breath. It's tough to be like them and I would only say that the very system which created them let them down. In the latter part of my career, I became very aware of who is what but I tried my best to design systems in such a way that an officer with questionable integrity was not allowed to breathe easy. Overt corruption, was made an example of and the officer in question was taken to task. But remarkably, some of the officers also corrected themselves with coaching and learnt to look at the larger picture. However, these numbers were too low for me to claim any real credit.

In my time in the police force, I have seen some remarkable justifications for bribery. Many policemen, especially of the lower ranks, justify their corrupt activity for their 'overwork' in the department. They claim—and rightfully so—that they work for upwards of fourteen hours a day and the pay they get for it is abysmal. The officers at the top level justify their corruption in terms of 'the missed opportunity cost'. They claim that their school and college peers are successful people now in terms of wealth and status and they are nowhere near them, so they want to make up for giving their time to the society. Both of these explanations border on absurdity as the human mind keeps defending the indefensible. They fail to understand that a job that requires service at its core can't be equated to market conditions outside. With jobs secure for life, with a comfortable salary and perks added to it and a life time pension, what more can one ask for?

The only saving grace is the genuine public respect and fulfilment that a honest guy gets and that is immeasurable. I can only say this as a closing comment. If a society lets down its good guys, it doesn't have any right to cry wolf when it suffers from bad governance. Identify the handful of good guys left in the system, start celebrating them and get them to positions where they can make a difference.

My mantras for winning the battle against bribery:

1. Create systems and practices specially at the recruitment stage to allow only the deserving ones in. If the entry itself is rotten, the bad effects can be only exponential.
2. Go after the corruption at the senior levels first so as to create a culture of excellence where good officers should thrive and not get suffocated.

3. Have an impartial 360-degree grading of the officer and have upright citizens carry out their performance reviews. Right now, the good grades the good, bad grades the bad and the inefficient grades the inefficient ones.
4. People to make their political leaders more accountable, even for officers' performance.
5. Insulate officer postings completely from the political set-up and the powers be including lobbies.
6. Citizens to get educated on petty corruption to enable a change in mindset. It's becoming very common to see citizens themselves offering a bribe even for genuine issues just to shorten a queue.

The Breed of Indian Politicians

Imagine the picture of a politician, preferably an Indian one. What is the first thing that comes to your mind? Let's be honest, you might have one or two favourites among them but you might probably hate them on the whole. This is no wonder as most of us see in an Indian politician everything that is wrong in our country, and sometimes everything that is wrong with us too.

I had the unique privilege of studying various types of politicians in close quarters. What started as an exercise in trying to do my job well later became an obsession to decipher what they were thinking and what motivated their actions.

The relationship between politicians and bureaucrats will always be an uneasy one. With one making the laws and the other implementing them, there is always bound to be that inevitable friction. Sometimes, with two strong alphas trying to guard their territories, skirmishes tend to occur on the field. Newspapers sometimes report on this, a big hullabaloo is made and we all go back to our own lives after the issue dies on its own. One of my initial interaction with a politician was almost comical and I just couldn't control my laughter once he left.

There was this ex-Member of the Legislative Assembly (MLA) who came to my office with about thirty odd people as one of his party workers was arrested for rioting. By then, as Assistant SP, I had built a reputation as a no-nonsense, tough officer and this person was very wary of talking to me directly. He made all of his party workers wait outside and came in. Once he was inside, the usual courtesies were exchanged and he beat around the bush without coming to the topic of discussion.

I asked him matter of factly, 'Sir, what can I do for you?'

He jumped on me energetically and spoke in a tone to indicate an intimacy both knew we did not share, 'ASP sir, you know nowadays people change MLAs the way they change TV channels. I have done such a good work for this constituency. But do people remember? By the time of elections they forget everything!'

He further rambled on, 'It's tough to be a politician in our country where people don't have any ethics'. I was losing my patience now and curtly asked him to come to the point.

With a rushed tone, he said 'I completely understand. My party workers were at fault. I have to support the law of the land to which you are indebted as well my party workers, to whom I'm indebted. Sir, please understand my party workers who are standing outside can't comprehend all of these things. They forced me to come here.'

It was a virtuoso performance from him till then but the killer line came next. Without blinking an eyelid, he said, 'Sir, since you understand my predicament, I kindly request you to come out with me and tell my workers that you have heard me and you will personally look into my request'.

I marvelled at his style of management and trying to do the impossible—to be in the good books of police and the party workers. I agreed to this as I felt there was nothing wrong in this. I walked out and told the assembled party men the same thing. They were fully elated and the leader also thanked me profusely and walked out. Later, we became excellent friends as we were both conscious of our boundaries and professional responsibilities.

This incident got me thinking on the fine line an Indian politician walks and the balancing act they have to indulge in to survive in our messy polity. To see an Indian politician in action is itself a spectacle. Nowhere in the world, can we see a politician thriving in the heat and dust like in our political theatre. The wins aren't guaranteed as the Indian election cycle is too complex to understand. The enemies are too many to count. The population, with its huge caste and other sociopolitical and economic dynamics seem to push politicians to the very edge. Elections have become extremely costly to run and the Election Commission equally tough to handle. With all of this, elections and politicians in India have truly become one of a kind.

In our democracy, with its 'first past the post' model in an ultra competitive electoral system, a politician needs to be seen in action all the time. If he cedes his space, there is always a competitor ready to take his spot. Some of his phone calls are courtesy ones to maintain friendships and connections with the police. A police officer gets several calls and requests for personal meetings from politicians. Many of the calls are harmless ones as the politicians tend to either reiterate what we have already done or what we will be doing. Some are the very rare kind of calls which are uncomfortable ones—they usually pertain to asking us to release one of their well-wishers or a follower or to water down the FIRs against them. From the tone and tenor, seasoned officers are usually able to understand whether they really mean what they are saying or if they are just posturing in front of their followers.

I took some time to decipher the game men in white were playing. Often, I used to wonder with hindsight that a politician I had a go at, could have been dealt with more deftly by me. More often than not, a politician in our democracy is a prisoner of his circumstances. Though they might appear insincere from the outside, when we make that extra effort to understand them, we might find a way to handle them. But when those politicians with whom I was rough, meet me at a later date, they behave as if nothing is amiss and I just couldn't find a way to become comfortable with them. For every rabble rouser and insincere one, I have also seen those who are thorough in their subject matter, are well-prepared for their meetings and demanding in the work they delegate to others. A significant number of politicians I have known belong to this category.

Some of my confusion around a politician's behaviour were cleared when I had an opportunity to catch up with a politician on a morning walk. That politician happened to be a sitting MLA of a district town, where I happened to serve as the SP. After the walk, he forced me to join him at his house, adjacent to the ground, for a cup of coffee. I relented, and when we reached his place I was astounded to see the sheer number of people waiting for him there—easily close to a hundred odd people. I understood later that this was his version of the *janata darshan* (people gathered to get their grievances addressed). Uncomfortable as I was, I still went in for that cup of coffee. I also asked him whether that big a crowd was a regular feature of his mornings. He said he saw close to 120 people on normal days. With my curiosity piqued, I told him that I was very interested in watching him interact with the people. He gamely agreed. What I saw for the next one hour changed my impression of public service in India and the role of politicians in it.

The lady who spoke to him first wanted some money to take care of her husband. With him in the sickbed and revenue sources running dry, she needed some urgent cash. There were many cases on municipal issues and some on the revenue authorities' side as well. There was also a case where a woman wanted the MLA to intervene and bring her son—who was sent to jail for stealing the batteries of a cell phone tower—back. Many of the requests were solely dependent on their perceptions of right & wrong and not based on the law. I saw the MLA handle most of the issues deftly for almost an hour. He even called up the local sub-inspector for a work which was not fully legal in its scope as well. He must have seen close to twenty-five people in an hour. His personal assistant had also quickly filtered out people and he made a couple of calls at his level to bring down the numbers. Invariably, all of them were offered *upma*, a south Indian breakfast and a cup of coffee and most people had their breakfast there. Later, when I wanted to leave, he offered to walk me out. I told him that I need to have a conversation with him about what I had seen.

A couple of days later, when he called me for other matters, we agreed to meet in my office and finish off what we had started. During the course of that discussion, I was able to understand the crazy life politicians lead and how people miss this thin line of a politician trying to balance the impossible demands of their constituents and delivering the needs with the inbuilt systemic inefficiencies. What I understood from that conversation was that people were likely to see the law as law when they were not personally affected. A woman whose son is arrested for a theft might not respect the law as, for her, her son takes precedence over everything else. With police stations not willing to listen to her completely illegal request, where could she go?

As a country that is in the process of improving its social security net by offering an economic cushion to the needy ones, a lot of people suffer simply because something bad has befallen them and they need that instant and immediate help. Most of the issues belonging to the public needs are matters that an efficient officer should be able to solve. With brokers rife in most government offices, even for genuine cases, people are forced to resort to a politician's support as they perceive them as people who can get the job done. In a faulty democracy, a politician becomes the go-to man for most people as he is most accessible and will get the job done for the immediate reward of their votes. When I asked him why did he call the sub-inspector, knowing fully well that his request was borderline illegal, he plainly answered that he just took his chance with that officer.

He further added that him not insisting on the same issue for a second time, with the officer by not following up, is a clear-cut signal he has given to the officer. Further, he clarified that over time, he had studied the officers well and knew exactly how to get the job done by them without being pushy. In short, I had seen a politician that day who was a master in dealing with people's emotions and adept at balancing the competing needs. This was the closest I came to a politician opening up to me and after a point, having closely followed several politicians of both the ruling and opposition parties, and I was able to pick up the nuances without them telling.

Later, in a separate context, another MLA similarly spoke to me of the daily expenses that he normally incurred. I instantly remembered the scene of breakfast being served in the previous story and told him about it. He was telling me how food played a major role in his house every day and later I gathered that many politicians have to run their houses like a canteen, serving breakfast, lunch and dinner. Though these are all very simple meals, they still had to cater to a couple of hundred people every day. This expense alone could run into a couple of lakhs every month. He also mentioned about the other 'incidental' expenses he was forced to partake in. According to his accounts, he visited an average of around ten marriage ceremonies every day in a wedding season, and multiple deaths every week. He was very careful to admit that the fact that he was attending at all was a burden to the host families as they would have to take care of his followers who usually mill around him, eating the food in the function as well. He would invariably gift about ₹5,000 to the newlyweds and help with ₹3,000 for a funeral. Throughout the year, depending on the season, his expenses would vary. During Ganesh Chaturthi, with over 500 pandals in his constituency, he would be giving anywhere from ₹5,000 to one lakh depending upon the scale of the function and the presence of his voters there. With close to fifty cricket and kabaddi matches in a year, he had to part with money for that. Church and mosque functions, depending on their importance, would require money too. Saying no to community leaders for any donation is tantamount to committing suicide because it will come back to bite the politician very strongly during elections as they have the power to swing a large number of community votes. In short, I could understand our faulty democracy at work here.

With different subsets of the population, each with their own aspirations and at various stages of economic growth, the Indian polity falls severely short in terms of where all of us need it to go. When a huge number of people are hanging around the politician in power, to take his spoils of office and redistribute it downwards, the chances of expecting the politician to behave like a model citizen is impossible, to say the least. Whether they mean to or not, the politician will always be the last man standing in our system as long as the people asking for their help have a voter ID card with them and are willing to trade their votes for the help.

I have also had the misfortune of meeting some of the absolutely rotten politicians. Their demeanour, language and thinking are, at least, a century old. They still maintain their hold on their constituency by utilising the fault lines of caste and the lack of exposure to the wider world of their people. All of them need to go, and undoubtedly, they will slowly go as the society has its own way of weeding out the bad ones.

Many of my batchmates and other officers would pull my leg about my closeness to many politicians and my ability to manage them well. I was also sent to the districts where I had previously worked when there were any major political flare-ups. One important thing that I used to tell my juniors was to try and understand the human side of the politicians well. Understanding the democracy from the surface level is important but more critical is to go a couple of levels deeper to see its actual workings. How do humans react when striped off their pretense? How do egos clash? How are leaders formed and destroyed in a matter of time?

Once we make it a habit to study people with all their complexities, it will really be easy for us to deal with our fellow beings, even politicians.

It was clear to me by now (as I hope it is to you) that all politicians aren't bad. In fact, I had seen an equal number of rotten officers as rotten politicians. There are officers who had made it a habit to sell almost all of their signatures with their integrity at the lowest. They are more threatening to the system as they directly lord over it without any adequate check and balance. I also felt it was always my duty to course correct politicians when they stepped completely out of line. I could do this with a well-meaning politician but not with an officer whose pay grade was way above mine. A bad politician was judged every five years at the ballot box and an officer none. The logic of interacting closely even with a bad politician is to make him see a better possibility for himself and for his electoral prospects.

I can categorise the interactions of the politicians with a civil servant into three parts—legal requests, requests bordering on illegality and blatantly illegal requests. Depending upon the nature of the requests they made, the tone and tenor with which I treated the politician also changed. If it was a legal request, they were more forceful as that request was made as a matter of right. I normally went all out to help him so that I could use the genuine favour as a bargaining chip later. For requests bordering on illegality, I tried and educated them on how their requests couldn't be carried out and even if they were, the actions had consequences. A simple example for this could be extending the timing of the loud speaker beyond 10 PM (most state laws stipulate it to be till 10 PM). I used to be very polite when denying a request as two angry minds on opposite sides would only create more havoc. Though practicality is much advised, once we start stretching a law, the bending happens sooner or later.

Any request that was blatant in nature was denied by me instantly. A firm no conveys a very strong message; I found that procrastinating on this by saying things like, 'I will look into it'; 'give me some time', 'I'll try my best', and other things, only built up undue expectations which only got busted in time. A firm no conveyed decisiveness which helped in future dealings. Whenever I got an opportunity to meet any unruly politician, I always made it a point to have a conversation about the blatantly illegal requests that were made and I tried and explained how it was problematic for everybody to act on it. One bad decision is enough to ruin any ones life built very meticulously. I always felt that conversations of this nature go a long way in building a good rapport.

My mantras for co-existing with a politician:

1. Understand politicians are not bad and they are the fulcrum that holds our democracy together.
2. Appreciate the dynamics he is working with. It could be castes, minority appeasement, majority backing, popularity or a closely-fought electoral area (which means a strong opposition candidate).

3. Find a common working relationship by not allowing perceptions to cloud either party.
4. Devise a strategy to deal with all requests—legal, bordering on illegal and blatantly illegal. Use different communication strategies for each.
5. Make it a habit to meet once in a while and over a point of time conversations can be on non-political subjects as well.
6. Still, if they are tough to handle and the government wants you out, go out with your dignity intact but not feeling bad. Some other people need your service more than that posting.
7. Never ever have an acrimonious thought even if transferred out unceremoniously. Any politician is a child of the forced circumstances, just wait for the overall quality of polity to improve.

Fighting the Underbelly of Our Society

It was a day that I won't forget in my life. After a day of hectic work, I was settling in for my typically late dinner at home when I got that much-dreaded emergency call. This was a call I was hoping that I should never get. In the evening I got to know as a matter of routine that a young girl named Diana,[1] who was in her tenth grade, was yet to reach home from her school. The girl was studying in a government school in one of the forested areas of our district. She was supposed to have reached her home at 6:30 PM and the parents intimated the police by 7:45 PM that she was nowhere to be found. The local officer also told me that they were checking with her friends, possible places she could have visited and they would get back once they had a lead. As expected, the parents and the villagers of that area were also actively searching for the missing girl.

Over the call, our inspector sounded alarmed and in a panicked voice said, 'Sir, we found the body of the girl'.

I could only mutter, 'Where?'

He continued with a bit more intensity, 'In the forest area between her school and home. Also, sir, we suspect she could have been sexually assaulted.'

With my blood-pressure rising, I stood up from my dinner table to wash my hands while simultaneously

[1] Name changed in order to protect the identity of the victim.

muttering instructions over the phone—asking enough forces to be mobilised, cordoning-off that area and securing the crime scene. I also told my officer to focus on his job and I would reach the spot as early as possible. With my mind racing and my driver racing through the streets, I was trying to piece together the puzzle and bracing for the worst.

The next seventy-two hours went in a daze. When I reached the spot, I couldn't go near the crime scene as the angry villagers gheraoed me and were baying for my blood. Somehow, I managed to go near the girl's body and could feel an array of emotions rushing through me. Primarily anger, for what had happened, and helplessness for the girl and her family. I was also washed over by a general sense of disbelief that incidents of this nature were still happening, but I had a more important job to do than worrying. It was time to control the crowd, take the body out to gather vital clues and to contain the law and order in the area.

With relay strikes by the students and the angry public on the roads, we had a tough time the next few days. Not only did we have to restore a sense of normalcy in the place, but we also had to crack the case in double quick time time, as most of our jobs were on the line. With multiple teams working, and thanks to our redoubtable investigators, we were able to crack the case and arrest the two juvenile criminals who were responsible. Post my interrogation of both the criminals, I was less excited about cracking this case and was more worried about the direction our society was (and still is) taking.

With the cremation done, the criminals sent to jail, tears shed and all the nice words spoken about the deceased girl whose only mistake happened to be being present at the wrong place at the wrong time, the only question I was asking myself was this: with the quick detection and arrest of the culprits and the police generally getting a good name, had we become a better society, a safer society, for women? Had we improved the general position of women in our society? My answer was an emphatic 'No'.

The unequal treatment of women begins at home. At school, a child is taught that all men and women are equal. If at home, fathers treat mothers in a way that society also silently endorses by not condoning, by hurling abuses, making them do all the household chores or treating them poorly, then a child's perception of their mothers is set in a particular mould. It is also starkly different from what they learn in school—that men and women are equal. That is not the reality they see before them.

Poor laws to effectively tackle domestic violence, is one of the most important reasons for violence against women being on the rise. With courts taking an extraordinarily long time to provide a civil remedy—like compensation to the women when they want to live away from their husbands for a while—how can we encourage women to come and report abuse at a police station or move away from their marital homes till they get their mental bearings right? So they continue to suffer in silence, trapped in the confines of abusive marriages, with parents who often refuse to take them back in.

Of late, I have seen the other end of this spectrum as well with married women, especially highly educated women. Visiting police stations within months of their marriage, preferring to file a complaint against their husbands and in-laws for domestic abuse or cruelty. When this issue gets enquired in detail, most often than not, it turns out to be a case of misunderstanding between the newlyweds, or in some cases, even cultural differences. It's pretty heartbreaking when our courts are flooded with cases of this nature and not genuine ones which ideally require our overburdened courts' time.

Empowerment begins at home. Parents have to teach their children to be worthy human beings. The onus is really on us. With parental norms taking a beating and children not getting rooted, most of the crimes, specially juveniles involving themselves in heinous crimes is only on an increasing trend.

If we start with Jyoti Singh's case in Delhi, which set in motion a series of measures in law and among the government agencies, or, more recently, Disha's case in Hyderabad, which produced an equally strong reaction (amongst others which either go unreported or do not find such a viral space in the media), one fact that stands out is this—most of the perpetrators of these gruesome crimes continue to be juveniles.

I have also seen enough number of juvenile criminals to understand this is only a growing menace. I had a rude awakening, with respect to Juvenile criminals, in one of the districts I had worked as police chief. One day, the police caught hold of a team of juvenile criminals who burgled a cooperative bank in a rural area. They entered the bank through the rooftop and emptied the iron safe which held cash and escaped the same way they had entered. When the police caught and brought them to me, I asked about their backgrounds and it turned out that they were mostly from broken families. With the procedures done and the perpetrators sent to juvenile homes, we thought that would be the end of the story. After a couple of months, another crime was committed with similar modus operandi (MO) in a nearby rural area. I told my officers to check for the same gang of juveniles. When we caught them again, I had decided to inspect deeper.

I visited each of their homes to look at their living conditions, their parents and the influence they were under so I could understand the psyche of these boys. Invariably, almost all the boys lived in shanties. Either their father or mother had left them at a young age and these kids had grown up without any supervision. They were growing up on their own, importantly, among the company of like-minded boys. Their sense of morality or right and wrong was drastically different from others. They had all started with small crimes, which went unreported and then gradually shifted to more serious crimes. More often than not, juvenile homes and jails only acted as a laboratory for them to mingle with like-minded criminals and make them fearless and brazen. These places also act as a university in the sense that they quickly learn the skillsets of bigger criminals and start implementing them with alacrity once they are out into the real world.

I also observed that their concept of somebody else's property was very different from how the law perceives it to be, their outlook on the 'weaker sex' far different from what you and I are taught. In short, their Dharma was different from ours. While the Mahabharata is taught to us from the perspectives of Krishna, Arjuna or even Duryodhana, they learnt it through the eyes of Shakuni. With not enough skills to get or hold down a job and on top of that, police records against them, they tended to turn to smaller crimes with a financial reward and gradually progressed to graver crimes that collectively shocked the conscience of our nation.

The solution for all of these is not only to progressively tighten our laws after every horrific crime but also to understand this requires a different approach. We have to start getting our social and economic interventions right to make sure all of these juveniles don't get the chance to turn criminals in the first place. It's true that we keep making the laws stricter with each passing day, like treating some of the juveniles as adults when trying them out in a court of law. All of these are demonstrable political commitments that build confidence in the public that their democracy is functioning. The Andhra Pradesh government has passed a law, post the Disha incident, mandating charge sheets to be filed within seven working days and the trial to be completed within fourteen working days from the date of filing the charge sheet. These are all emergency measures that were needed to assuage the public anger. But the acts that will create the long-term impact are the ones that will create less fanfare and might not offer instant political mileage like weaning these youths off a life of crime.

India is a country that is sitting on a powder keg of youths—economists might choose to call this a demographic dividend. Whether this turns out to be a demographic disaster purely depends on the country's will and its ultimate success in making all of these youths gainfully employed. With universities and colleges churning out graduates at an unbelievable rate, many of whom are poorly trained and skilled, it looks like we might not be able to give wings to all of these youths' dreams in the near future. According to an estimate from TeamLease,[2] close to eighty per cent of engineers from long tail institutes (institutions ranked above fifty-one) and ninety-nine per cent of management graduates from long tail institutes are not up to the mark in terms of skillset and employment is not possible for them. The same estimate also states that close to sixty per cent of 3.5 lakh management graduates don't find a management job. Ironically, the same report talks of a labour deficit in vocational job markets which is all set to balloon to 41.4 to 61.4 million vacancies in the next five years. With less emphasis on vocational and diploma courses (as many of us take that as a prestige marker) we are missing out on a huge opportunity to create jobs and gainfully employ millions. Imagine a country creating employment in this job space for millions and taking pride in it. If we are not able to take care of our inner-city kids, how are we going to take care of our outer city kids and rural graduates?

I have also seen in German police stations where there is a position of a youth police officer. The job of this officer is to profile youths living in slightly far off or inaccessible areas, youth living close to closed steel mills or any other industrial establishments and to find a way to connect with them. This can go as far as a job referral

[2] Monit Khanna. 'Being An Electrician Pays More Than An Engineer Or MBA Job With Same Experience, Reveals Study'. *IndiaTimes*, 17 December 2019. https://www.indiatimes.com/technology/news/survey-reveals-people-pick-mba-engineering-even-when-jobs-like-gemologist-electrician-pay-a-lot-more-502501.html

for potential jobs for them. Also, the major German football clubs take extra interest in encouraging all these youths to enroll for football matches and mingle with their stars. We also have seen major English football clubs having the same sort of approach in some of the English cities. I know it sounds and looks daunting in a setting like an Indian city with its huge population and myriad of problems. But time has come to find an interlinked solution to all of these. The poor quality of education is leading to poor graduates who don't get employed and this creates a social unrest sooner or later. With no emphasis on diplomas or vocational training, we are missing out on the grey collar economy that India is uniquely positioned to create with its millions of potential graduates.

Most of the Indian cities are bursting at their seams while some are transforming into mega cities of the world. Reports say that India is home to close to five out of thirty-seven megacities in the world.[3] With the growth of population in cities, all of us are also becoming anonymous. In a village, everyone knows everyone and any new outsider is easily found out. With agriculture dying a slow death and the great Indian migration happening at a rate that is faster than any recorded migration in its history, cities have become unlivable and crime-infested.[4] I have seen this pattern when I had

[3] The World's Cities in 2016, *United Nations*. https://www.un.org/en/development/desa/population/publications/pdf/urbanization/the_worlds_cities_in_2016_data_booklet.pdf

[4] Divay Pranav. 'India preparing for the biggest human migration on the planet', *India Invest*, 2 January 2018. https://www.investindia.gov.in/team-india-blogs/india-preparing-biggest-human-migration-planet

one stint as a deputy commissioner with the Bengaluru city police. The kind of lawlessness we see on the streets like chain-snatching, bag-and-mobile phone-snatching and knifing (even to take ₹50 from a victim's pocket) are only on a rise. Most of the criminals, as usual, are juveniles or are below thirty years of age. With the lifestyle of a city that values and rewards the culture of instant self-gratification, we have the have-not's who wants to mimic the have's and the have's who want to mimic a lifestyle that requires them to splurge money that is not of their own earning.

The issue of the free availability of porn videos and the revenge porn videos that is in circulation is also a huge cause for concern. The average Indian consumed 11GB data per month in 2019, which is about a forty-seven per cent increase over the previous year and is growing exponentially.[5] Now, the question to be asked is whether all this browsing has made our lives productive or whether the youth is fully immersed into this online world that is encouraging them to commit some of these acts in the real world? No empirical study worth its salt has come out with a firm conclusion.

With a sense of anonymity in the big city, they get encouraged to commit crimes and continue with more crimes once they come out after serving their sentence. That's why the number of 'repeat offenders' is at an all-time high. When you ask a repeat offender the question—'Why have you brazenly committed the crime with no fear of the law?'— their answer is almost always the same: 'Since we are trapped in this lifestyle, we see no way out.' With one crime committed and their names in the local police database, they are all but doomed as chances of them getting a job become close to zilch because of the negative police verification report. To come out of the jail on bail, they have to shell out an upward of ₹40,000 to their lawyers. To pay back that money that they have borrowed, they go on a crime spree. That's why the biggest criminal lawyers are so busy—they have a lot of people to argue for.

Lastly, with the emergence of new slums or some of the urban settlements having the characteristics of

[5] Nokia - Annual Mobile Broadband India Traffic Index (MBiT) report -2020.

a slum, people live very close to each other. These are all congested areas that breed a sense of false security to them as they become part of in-groups. With cities expanding and the costs of living increasing exponentially, some of these areas emerge as hotspots for youths to live and build a network. These are the areas that need urgent attention from the civic agencies, the local government and the police to try and help these youths lead an honest life.

> *The instant case manifests the multitudes of restrictions and taboos with which women in rural areas are brought up, grow and survive. It epitomizes the fear ingrained in the mind of a young girl in the countryside or elsewhere against reporting the issues of sexual assault of powerful adults.*
>
> —From the judgment of the District Sessions Court in Delhi holding a sitting MLA of Uttar Pradesh guilty for abducting and raping a victim from Unnao.

There was a case of a sixteen-year-old victim who was abducted and raped by a sitting MLA of the ruling party in Uttar Pradesh. The victim finally managed to file a complaint after two months and ten days. With a herculean effort, the alleged accused and the local MLA were included in the FIR. Later, the victim's father was allegedly framed in an Arms Act case and sent to jail on 3 April 2018 and he died a few days later on 9 April under inexplicable circumstances while in judicial custody. The coincidences were only beginning. The victim, on 28 July 2019, while going in a car along with her aunts and lawyer was hit by a lorry and two of her aunts died. After a nation-wide public outcry, the victim was shifted to AIIMS for her medical treatment. After the Honourable Supreme Court's intervention, the case was transferred to a court in Delhi and away from Lucknow. The CBI had taken over the investigation, and the chargesheet was filed only on 3 October 2019. After a daily hearing of this case, the Delhi District and Sessions Court delivered its judgment on 16 December 2019. It held the sitting MLA guilty of raping the victim.

One of the most common, if not misplaced, complaint we hear is about the application of law selectively vis-a-vis a powerful accused and a powerless victim. In this case, the victim had to overcome a powerful patriarchal mindset of her village. As if that weren't enough, she also had a powerful political leader as the main accused. Not only did she have to fight her case, but also had to overcome several personal obstacles including losing her father, her two aunts and almost losing her life itself.

This story holds good across Indian states—whether it be a powerful business man who burns his victim in a tandoor at an upscale pub in Delhi or a powerful politician's son arm-twisting the law to escape from the rape and murder of a victim. The instances are very many but the nature of the victim is almost the same. The victim is most often a poor, rural girl who has to go through heavy dose of character assassination when the trail is on, has to jump through several hoops and finally only gets the justice when there is strong public outcry forcing all the agencies to wake up and work at break neck speed.

In this case, the judge also added, 'In my considered opinion, the investigation has suffered from patriarchal approach or inherent outlook to brush the issues of sexual violence against children under the carpet apart from exhibiting lack of sensitivity and humane approach. It appears that somewhere investigation in the instant case has not been fair for the victim of the crime and her family members.'[6]

I have also seen this apathy in the rural areas during my surprise inspections of police station there. I invariably saw a group of women or a family sitting outside and wailing. When I would ask them what the issue was, the answer would usually be that a girl was missing for some hours or in some cases even days. On speaking to the Station House Officer (SHO), the answers I received would be something like:

'Sir, she must have run away with somebody and she will come back after a couple of days.'

'Sir, the locals have seen the girl talking to some boy outside her college. She should be safe with that boy.'

Or, a completely unacceptable police version like

'Sir, the parents are lying to hide something, we need to enquire in detail to find out the truth.'

This perfectly brings out the apathy we have and the mindset that resides in the inner most recess of our brain. It takes enormous amount of painstaking work to help the policemen to come out of this mindset. Mainly, promptly attending to this kind of cases gives

[6] *The Hindu*. 'Kuldeep Sengar held guilty in Unnao minor rape case', *The Hindu*, 16 December 2019. https://www.thehindu.com/news/national/other-states/kuldeep-sengar-convicted-in-unnao-rape-case/article30319473.ece

us that initial time to quickly put our resources to the job at hand before something terribly goes wrong as in Disha's rape and murder case in Hyderabad where the victim's family ran around three police stations in the middle of the night to get the correct jurisdiction of the crime.

In the case of the sexual assault and murder of the girl, Diana, I had found out the following after my emotions had settled.

Diana was at the wrong place and at the wrong time on that particular day. She only died on that day because some of the societal and economic forces were against her. Her friends, who normally accompanied her from her home in the morning and back to her home in the evening, had left early on that fateful day as Diana was supposed to attend a computer class at 6:00 PM. With only one functioning computer for the whole school and the computer time getting rationed, she got her chance only at 6:00 PM and by that time, her friends had left for the village. When she finished her assignment at 6:30 PM, she started walking the 5.3 km distance by road all alone. Out of this, close to 3 km was a forest-covered route. The accused were lying in wait for any girl who would happen to cross that route at that point of time. One against three, with an unforgiving terrain also against her, she literally had zero chances of defending herself. As predicted, the two juveniles came from broken families and lived in areas close to each other. One of the boy was growing up without a father and one without a mother. The criminals were of the opinion that the girl wouldn't fight with them and would walk off silently. Since she fought back with them she was butchered brutally.

The only question I can ask then and now is, what if? What if the state had taken care to provide the school with enough computers? What if the state had provided buses on that route no matter the profit-loss margin? What if the juveniles came from well-settled families that kept them in check?

Diana, who died on 17 June 2015, had topped her school in her tenth standard exams and was looking forward to being a doctor. She died for no fault of her own like most young girls of her age. She died because the society failed her that day, as it had every day since her birth.

Dharma and Law—The Daily Struggle

The policeman in India is expected to enforce the law of the land and are expected to do it freely, fairly and fearlessly. To this end, they are guided by the statute books and other penal laws that the lawmakers had codified. This shift took place when the British crown took hold of Indian affairs, and so, instead of a small group of chosen people rendering justice, the system that is in existence now is codified in the form of statutes. The common denominator between the two systems was the upholding of Dharma. Though it appears easy, implementation of Dharma in sync with the law of the land is a daily struggle a policeman has to face.

Dharma is a complex word to define and generally it is understood as an individual's duty fulfilled by observance of custom or law. It's also a sense of righteousness. Dharma essentially means 'doing things the right way'. There is a Dharma for a justice–giver and likewise, there is a Dharma for a victim. All man-made laws are derived majorly from natural and universal laws. All of the laws are works in progress and keep evolving. In the olden times, before the introduction of the policeman and codified laws, how was justice served? We are talking about a period before 1850. Most often, the village elders would be the final arbiters of justice. Both petty cases and serious cases like murder would be taken before them and the jury assembled would inquire into all the versions of the story to arrive at a decision. Sometimes, it would be an eye for an eye. Even in the highest of the king's courts, this was the system and procedure. When codified laws came in, our society ceded some powers to the state that was created to look after them. Previously, people had the right to kill somebody when someone close to them got killed by the person in question. With the invention of nation states, many crimes like murder were categorised as state crimes and the state was put in charge of those.

Also, the laws need to be frequently amended to stay in tune with society's evolution and progress. Major amendments do happen, bowing down to the will of the people, like classifying certain categories of crimes committed by a minor to be tried by the laws applicable to an adult. While it's understood that policemen are expected to implement the laws in letter and spirit, without a correct understanding of Dharma, the application often goes haywire. If we go right back to the first codified laws, we would be guided by the Hammurabi code of justice.[1] There were two important factors for the consideration of punishment. First, the certainty of it, and second, the actual delivery of it. Simply put, a punishment needed to be meted out within a certain time period and it had to be given out in a proper form, depending on the nature of the offence. In the whole process, Dharma had to be met. In a country like India, with our operating philosophy of justice,

[1] The Hammurabi code of laws is a well-preserved Babylonian code of law of ancient Mesopotamia, dated to about 1754 CE. It is a collection of 282 written laws (from www.history.com).

there are several cases in which certainty is not met with. Because of this, a few innocents might languish in jail along with a large number of accused who are whiling away their time there, while their victim suffer outside. Here, the Dharma is definitely not meted out.

Since the emphasis is on making sure not even a single innocent gets punished, that extra bit of time is required by our Indian system, unlike a jury trial or a plea-bargaining system. In this, one of the very important components is the initial charge, in the form of a chargesheet, made out by the police on behalf of the state. Be it any kind of case from a grievous one like the rape and murder to the non-grievous ones like an assault or a petty fight, a chargesheet is filed. This is purely the version of the police, on behalf of the state, after the investigation is done. The subsequent trials from a local court all the way to the Supreme Court, are purely dependent on the application of mind and the sense of balance applied by the police officer when deciding on the merits of the case. This part (of finding out to what degree the charge is correct) is often overlooked when trying to decide on the merits of the case. Usually, the policemen apply the law in its entirety without worrying too much about the inherent contradictions of the versions of truth itself. Though there is a court available to see that and hear out the different parties, this is a daily struggle for a conscientious police officer.

The law is not only merely applying the procedural aspects that are mentioned in a law book but bringing it closer to Dharma while doing it. The supervisory officer has to make sure that the law is applied well and satisfies the objective it was directed towards. That is the officer's Dharma. This was always a struggle for me in my daily job because the information, by the time it reached me, was heavily filtered and the version of truth was also varnished with a tinge of police flavour to it.

Though the focus is completely on the victim of a crime, in many cases my primary duty was to take care of my own people when they are in trouble. For an officer one of the biggest nightmares is when an accused dies in our police custody. Worst still when it happens inside the police station. Lock-up deaths are interpreted in many ways, but the most common interpretation is a scenario where it is assumed that the policemen have themselves killed a person under custody. Policemen-turning-killers cannot be condoned and they deserve the strictest punishment. But a large percentage of cases happen, when the accused person commits suicide inside the station premises and this is also classified as a lock-up death. A large percentage of cases happen, when the accused person commits suicide inside the station premise; this is also classified as a lock-up death. With the National Human Rights Commission (NHRC) being very strict on lockup deaths now, there is a whole host of Standard Operating Procedures (SOPs) at play. Importantly, it also generates a huge amount of friction with the local public and in many instances, the agitating public have burned down a police station or worse still, killed police personnel themselves.

When I was serving as the Superintendent of Police (SP) in my first district I was informed of a lock-up death. I immediately rushed to the police station to get a first-hand account of what had happened. I was hoping for the worst, as I had only read about the cases till then but had not experienced one personally. This was a case of our local police arresting a person in the middle of the night for assaulting his wife. He was drunk as well. Immediately after bringing him to the station, they kept him in the lock-up cell and gave him food. Our law allows our policemen to hold a suspect in custody for twenty-four hours before they can be produced before a court of law. In the middle of the night, when the suspect asked for a bedsheet as he was feeling cold, the local police promptly gave him one. Within a couple of hours, when the night in-charge officer checked on the accused, he found the accused had committed suicide by hanging himself—the bedsheet was tied to the toilet pipe inside the lock up. Desperate men find desperate measures to commit suicide and this was one. All hell broke loose in the morning, when the accused's relatives swarmed the station, accusing the local police of murdering the man. Not only was this a major law and order issue, but the local politicians were also mingling with the crowds and instigating them. Their demands were a job for a family member of the dead accused, a cash compensation and action against the police.

I consulted with the collector (administrative head) of the district as he was to give a report to the NHRC. He simply asked me to suspend the in-charge officer of the station, who in this case, was an inspector. He said, prima facie we could show the NHRC our sincerity in trying to get to the bottom of this episode and also calm the public. This was the easiest option for most of us and even the inspector was on board with this. He was also convincing himself that they shouldn't have given the bedsheet to the accused. I was very clear that a part of the law could be satisfied by placing the officer under suspension but no part of Dharma would be satisfied here. After due consideration, I was of the firm opinion that the police did their job and there was no question of taking any action against them, come what may. I made my stand very clear to the collector and to my immediate supervisory officer, an Inspector General of Police (IG). Later, with firmness and decisiveness, we were able to convince and disperse the assembled crowd as well. I had to go through a tough time for this as I was personally summoned by the NHRC to explain my actions as well as the enquiry that was conducted by the state government through the Criminal Investigation Department (CID). I'm stating this incident to merely convey a point of the inherent struggle one has to go through to keep alive Dharma in its true spirit.

Dharma to a larger extent depends on the perception of the different affected parties. Not only should justice get served, but it should also appear to be served. Different perceptions arise when the information flow is curtailed and people don't get complete information of the issue at play. In the above mentioned case, the information victim's family had was completely different as they might not have believed the story of a policeman giving a bedsheet as the image of the police among the public is entirely different. In the case of senior officers, we will also see our men with a sense of distrust. The same is true of the different stakeholders as well. Naturally, truth gets filtered out and we start making decisions that are convenient and easy to sell. I eventually understood the best way for Dharma to be rooted is when information is made free and we become totally transparent. This should border on radical transparency. When we advocate it and follow scrupulously, the mirage of Dharma can be made visible to a common eye.

For me, the other issues of confrontation were to be in the Road Traffic Accident (RTAs) cases. With India quickly becoming the accident capital of the world, the dilemmas used to be plenty. The common practice is to label the driver of the larger vehicle as the accused and that of a smaller vehicle as the victim. Most often, the guy in the smaller vehicle would be economically not well-to-do and the family would have lost their only bread-earner. I used to break this practice with a very heavy heart. Dharma, in my opinion, is not helping the weaker guy. Of course, they need to be helped but not at the cost of the stronger guy when the weaker guy is at fault. Insurance money being paid by companies for no fault of their client due to incorrect classification by the police is against the law—it is adharma. Many policemen and the family members of the deceased used to be very unhappy with me for this, but with a heavy heart I did it anyway.

These are the daily struggles and a sense of helplessness that almost cut through to our bones. The same yard stick I used to apply for most of the cases of police assault as well as public assaulting a policeman. There are cases where the policemen are clearly at fault, they would have provoked a civilian and they would have reacted to that. Our policemen would have booked him under the section that is reserved for assaulting a public servant in duty and would be ready to send him to jail. These kind of cases, I would be forcibly intervening to save that person, arguing it is not Dharma on our part to use our power on the hapless and on the weak.

In the later part of my police career, when I was posted to a metropolitan district, as its deputy commissioner, I had to make a very unusual and possibly one of the toughest decisions of my career. This is a case of one of the stations under my watch that was getting into frequent troubles and catching the media's attention as well. The officer who was in charge previously had also tried his best to control the situation. There was a case of the weapon inside the station that went missing and later it was found that one group had taken it to take revenge on the other group. During my tenure, when I got the information that the same station is divided along caste lines, region and age groupwise, I visited them and gave one last warning. The final straw on the proverbial camel's back was when a citizen was severely assaulted in that station premises and we all felt ashamed of it. I called my local ACP to discuss the options available to us and I decided to go for the boldest move possible and that was never attempted in that unit's history. I decided to recommend to the commissioner of police to transfer the whole station of 71 personnel. When my ACP said, that might not be right, I remember clearly telling him that each personnel is responsible for allowing the station culture to get spoilt. Either they could have played an active role by being part of one of the various groups which constitutes the commission of a wrong or by not trying to report to us, they are a part of an omission by failing to maintain the mandatory team spirit. Later, I convinced the commissioner and transferred all of them out. One of the station personnel who was on leave that day also died because of heart attack. When the media tried linking his death to my action, I was very clear in my heart, my act was without any prejudice and was for the betterment of the policing. If the station is itself divided, how can we be expected to give good policing by standing united. Later, I met all the staff members, explained my actions to them and hosted them over a dinner and saw them off. These are all daily struggles most of us had to go through by being very careful with our actions and also being very conscious of making sure our lethal powers are used within a proper context by not causing any harm to the innocent. If you ask me, whether I would have used my powers a hundred per cent the right way, I can only say I acted every time with absolute integrity. I also should have the humility to admit that some of my actions could have caused some harm to somebody because of incorrect interpretation of the situation or with a wrong information being fed to me but never with a mala fide intent.

India, off late, is seeing police encounter death cases that are sensational in nature. Like in the case of four accused being shot dead while allegedly escaping custody in a southern Indian state. Here, they were accused of one of the worst possible crimes against a fellow human being—of committing a rape and later burning the victim. In another case, in the northern part of India, it was gang lords who had a falling out with the system. We have seen a cinematic-style killing of policemen by a group of daring criminals and the subsequent police action where the top criminal himself was killed after he was taken to custody. When we see the public's reaction to this, they are joyful and seem to have a total sense of acceptance. In some cases, the jubilant public have showered flower petals on the concerned policeman. The cops are feted as heroes and an 'encounter specialist' tag is attached to them for eternity. We have seen this in different metropolitan cities as well, when criminals reared their heads at different points of time. We also have cases of similar nature across the major cities of India but don't garner enough national attention to be a talking point for a couple of days. When one goes to the reasons of why this is happening, the convenient answer that is always given is the 'implementation of Dharma'. This is also a time to question the fairness of that argument.

A criminal is shaped gradually by a variety of circumstances—the lack of legitimate opportunities, the system of caste and other factors, in-built intelligence, daringness, co-opting the governmental systems and sometimes plain luck. Once they grow to a certain level, they enter into the category 'too big to fall'. That's when encounter deaths happen. Though we are not party to the actual circumstances of the above-mentioned cases, we are in a position to understand what could have happened by piecing things together. Imagine the plight of the public who don't get treated fairly by the same system. When they go to the police station for any common issue, they fall into the category 'too small to fall'. That's when they get the abuses, the kicks and the beatings. This is where many of the human rights violations start as well. The policeman becomes a final arbiter of law and they start meting out instant punishment believing it is their duty. The logic is that by doing this they are not burdening the courts and giving instant succour to the victims. Sometimes, it could be a simple slap to bring a dispute to rest, but at other times, it may well be a volley of bullets. If one section of the government becomes the final dispenser of justice without adequate check and balance, we will soon enter into anarchy. We all know what thrives in anarchy—a sense of lawlessness and favouring the mighty over who is right. To do that we have to be very disciplined in our usage of the word Dharma. The courts are the final arbiters of justice and they have a balanced dharmic perspective between the victim, the accused and their rights and wrongs. That's why the focus should always be on thorough investigation, careful building of facts and its presentation to a court, proper follow-up of the case and not giving up even if it takes time. By doing this, not only are we going after the criminals but also after their network. The network that had sustained the criminal so strongly till then, will quickly sprout out a newer criminal, much faster than the time it took for an older one to vanish away. This is the basic problem when we confuse Dharma with an uncluttered mind that seeks instant and immediate gratification.

It's a constant striving to catch that mirage of Dharma with all our inbuilt sense of prejudice and sense of self-importance. It is also that striving that keeps moving us and our job towards that impossible perfection. So let us continue to live and enjoy that striving.

> Conflict pushes a human being to deviate from 'being human'. Human beings, being social and collaborative in nature, are in perpetual competition in the name of modern civilisation. Conflict stems from one's insecurity and lack of faith in one's true nature and in the true nature of the world around us.

Law, by its very nature, simplifies most of this human conflict to a mere black and white phenomenon. Application of it is also bound to have times when the real justice might slip through the cracks. Dharma, on the other hand, is dependent purely on the consciousness level of the human beings present in a society, where everyone feels wanted and safe.

Dharma is the absence of somebody progressing only because they were born into a particular background; the systems being rigged against the weak and the powerless. True Dharma is an endless work in progress and striving for it makes our lives meaningful.

THE FACELESS HEROES

—The men and women who truly matter

The Go-Getters

Wilfred Pareto, an Italian economist turned sociologist, in the late 1890s popularised the concept of 'Pareto's Principle' in which he talked about his 80:20 ratio. Initially, he used his theory for the economic elites to measure income distribution. Later, in his work as a sociologist, this principle was expanded to other fields—most notably, management. He predicted that eighty per cent of effects come from twenty per cent of causes. By an extension of the same logic with my experience, I saw that eighty per cent of the results of the organisation were contributed by twenty per cent of its human resources.

This latter group comprised of the critical individuals without whom we would see an instant drop in the overall performance of the company. Nowhere have I seen this principle more in play than in our police forces. The critical twenty per cent at all levels are the go-getters for me. They go to any level to get the job done and they don't allow their career prospects and family compulsions to come in the way of what they can deliver. In this chapter, I would like to introduce some of these men and women and their mindset to you.

Some officers in the force are more efficient than the others, more caring than their average group and most importantly, have a greater sense of purpose than the rest. Police work under normal circumstances itself is very taxing and when extraordinary circumstances arise, we can easily make out the chaff from the wheat. With law and order situations on the rise, it goes without saying that a policeman rushes headlong into the danger. More often than not, it's the officers who rush head-on as there usually is not much time to wait for better data and decide. With lives at stake, especially in communal riots, there is no other option but to embrace the danger voluntarily. I have seen this in action very tellingly with Indian Armed Forces. During my interactions with some of the army personnel, I have learned this important lesson and I'm reproducing a typical conversation here.

'*Saab*, you fight for your country?'

'Yes sir, I fight for my country but more important than that, I fight for my unit.'

'Why unit?'

'It's my pride. And not only that sir, I will fight for my captain till my last breath.'

'Why is that, *saab*?'

'Sir, you might not understand if I explain this to you. You got to see how we live, how we train, how we play and most importantly, how we fight. I welcome you to visit us.'

I have seen this uniformly across different army units during my field attachments from Assam to Nagaland and in the plains of Jhansi. I have made it a mission to understand this phenomenon totally and to derive lessons, if any. The aim was to replicate the same culture, or at least a part of it, in our daily lives.

The institution of Armed Forces is perhaps a very unique example of an organisation centred on personal leadership. The officers lead the way and it starts with their selection process. With a rigorous process, lasting days, only the very best of those who exhibit personal leadership abilities are allowed to get in. The training standards emphasise and reiterate that. Immediately after training, in their very first posting as captains, there are allocated to a regiment and usually are expected to stay with that regiment throughout their service. As young men, they get embedded into a unit, stay with their men, dine with them and lead them from the front. I remember the many letters we received at my SP office from very senior leaders like Captains, Lieutenant Colonels and sometimes even Colonels, about the problem a member of their unit was facing. Most often it was a unit member's family issue back home and they wanted us to address it, which we promptly did.

To truly understand how our officers lead their men by example, we need only observe the ratio of officers to soldiers who die in major wars. After the Kargil war ended and as per the report given by an army spokesperson,[1] we know that in the Kargil war, the ratio was 1:17, in the 1965 war it was 1:18, in the 1971 war it was 1:20. Heart wrenchingly, in the last major war India fought, the Kargil war, we lost twenty-six officers and 527 soldiers.[2] This is the price brave men

[1] Aniruddha Bahal. Nitin A Gokhale, Dras. 'Leading From The Front', *Outlook*, 26 July 1999. https://www.outlookindia.com/magazine/story/leading-from-the-front/207810

[2] *The Times of India*. 'Kargil war victory came at cost of young officers' lives', *The Times of India*, 27 July 2018. https://timesofindia.indiatimes.com/city/shimla/kargil-war-victory-came-at-cost-of-young-officers-lives/articleshow/65156171.cms

pay for leading and putting the nation first. Since the officers take care of their men like family and stand by them, the men, over time, develop that intimate sense of belonging to their unit just like their family. In any case, they tend to spend more time with the units than their families during their careers.

Replicating this in a police set-up is very tough as in a civilian field like ours, the selection process is not as rigorous as in the army for officers, even for IPS officers. We are tested more for our knowledge and our attitude to work in a democratic set-up. Naturally, here the nature of leadership mettle cannot be of the same standard as in the army but once in a while, when we see leadership of a very fine quality in the field, all we have to do is latch on to them and give them our support and protection whenever we needed to. In a batch of young sub-inspectors' (SI), immediately after their training, they are given their field postings. We, as senior officers, would be looking forward to their arrival as they bring that breath of fresh air to the worn-out legs in the field. We worry about shaping them up well and they are normally attached to good police stations where the culture of policing and the officers who lead those stations are up to the mark.

If we can shape their formative years right, then we get jewels among us. They do not allow unnecessary things to tempt them, spoils of their offices to corrupt them and they have that beginner's spirit and zeal for years. But sadly, we lose out a significant number very quickly. Many are lost to the temptations that young minds such as theirs find hard to resist and they quickly go some of their seniors' way. The few who continue to fight their worst impulses, suffer enormously in their careers for the simple fact that they are unafraid to say 'No' to the powers that be—they are the Pareto's twenty per cent. They are the people—be it officers or men—who continue to improve the standards of policing, carry this institutional knowledge, hand it over to the next generation and maintain the moral fabric of their uniform. I have been privileged and honoured to meet quite a few of those officers during their service. The following stories are about them—those who were much better than I could ever even aspire to be. Though there are many remarkable stories, I have taken a couple of them to bring these officers and men alive here.

Once I had to send an officer and his team up till Nepal chasing a criminal gang who was on the run with the looted booty. This was a race against time and our initial investigation had shown us that this gang might be moving towards Nepal. This case was so dynamic that no definite playbook could be used and our team was given complete autonomy to execute the mission. Since we didn't have any idea of the route that the criminal gang will take, this team had to further split into multiple teams and travel by multiple routes and different modes of transport. They had to cover all the entry points to Nepal for ten days, checking every vehicle and luggage for the culprit and the booty. They returned after twenty-seven days with the accused, who had been nabbed after chasing him throughout the country in trains, buses, auto rickshaws and even in a bullock cart!

With government support not being available on crucial fronts like finances, they were on their own, holding on to the mission and staying motivated. This, for me, is priceless. We can talk about and teach leadership or even take credit, but the output is derived only when the rubber meets the road. We just have to imagine the ordeal they must have gone through in foreign territory with nobody to look after them except themselves. It is also a fact that the whole team just left at a moment's notice given by me. They just went to their houses, packed their bags and informed their loved ones that they were leaving to a location for their duty. If their loved ones had asked them when they were likely to be back, their answers most likely would have been, 'I don't know, whenever the job is over'. I believe this needs a remarkable mindset and a sense of duty. But this is the daily ordeal some of these go-getters go through. We are also overly dependent on them and unsurprisingly, they take the bulk of our loads.

In the middle of this ordeal, my sub-inspector called me to inform that his mother was hospitalised with a possibility of her being diagnosed with cancer. I urged him to start homeward immediately and told him that I'll send a replacement officer at the soonest. What he told me in response will remain etched in my memory till my last breath as a constant reminder to 'focus on the job at hand'. He said, 'Sir, I'm pursuing an important lead in Mumbai and will move towards Pali, Rajasthan. My replacement officer will take some time to understand this and start the work. In that time that is lost, the lead will go cold. Let me stay and complete the mission. You please do me a favour. Just make sure my mom is taken care and the Arogya Bhaghya Yojane letter is issued on priority basis. That's the only request sir.'

Arogya Bhagya Yojane is a well-acknowledged benefit that the Karnataka government gives its policemen to cover them and their family for their medical needs. As tears welled up my eyes, I wasn't sure if I would have done the same thing under similar circumstances. This ability to see the big picture by keeping the emotions out, being objective and fully focused on the mission is a trait that an Indian policeman possesses with great pride. By no stretch am I advising this was the correct course for anyone. I'm just trying to illustrate that we have men of this kind of mettle with us to protect and serve us.

With pesky calls to our mobile phones on the rise and many innocents losing their hard-earned money to scams, in one of our meetings a young sub-inspector proposed an idea which was as daring as the mission itself. He had located the caller, after cracking the accused's internet calls, to a place in Jharkhand. He said he wanted to go and nab this gang. My first concern was my team's safety and secondly the operational challenges this would entail. He convinced me with his plan and embarked on a train journey to Jharkhand along with his small team. After reaching the state capital, he further travelled to the small town and surveyed the area to zero down the location. With continuous effort for a couple of days, he located the building from which the accused and his team were operating. He went inside like a sales person and got to know that it's a sophisticated call centre with close to thirty employees and separate 'business units', if I may call them so, for languages like Hindi, English, Kannada, Tamil, Telugu and Malayalam. Their whole operation was a fraud of the highest order, conning the unsuspecting by making them divert their money into the accounts of the culprits, in real time.

Our officer had done everything till then by risking his life as well. The toughest challenge for him now was to convince the ecosystem around him to do its job. He took on the job then of convincing the reluctant local police into supporting him and the team. With a skeleton team, comprising of our men and the local police, he raided the centre, took everybody into custody and seized all electronic evidences. The scene that followed this remarkable deed seemed to be straight out of a Bollywood movie. The local population, not wanting the local police to cooperate with our police team, gheraoed them and surrounded the local police station.

The local public wanted all the arrested to be set free and our team to be sent back to Karnataka. Senior police officers from both states intervened and finally the necessary support was extended at the police station to follow the procedures as established by law. When the accused gang was taken to the local court for a remand order, the lawyers teamed up there against our men as well. Our sub-inspector argued in front of the Honourable Judge with the minimal Hindi he knew and stood his ground. After a marathon hearing with noisy protests by the local lawyers, he successfully took orders to take the gang into custody and obtained a transit warrant to bring them to our police headquarters.

When the team and the gang were all set to return, he called me with a request. He said, 'Sir, everything is done now. Can you coordinate with the Indian Railways and get them to give us a full compartment to transport all the accused? This bogey needs to be attached to the train. I have done the paper work as well and if you call them, they might feel happy and our file might move faster.' This act of doing everything on their own and leaving the small insignificant things to us was not new to me. This was the only help they expected from us where we needed to put the weight of our office to get some urgent things done. The Indian Railways was kind enough to accept our request on priority and sanctioned an entire coupe for our team. An operation of this kind in an alien state that required convincing multiple stakeholders against all odds— police, courts, local population, political leaders, railways— made this one of the favourite events of my police career. As it's often said, for every bad incident involving a police and becoming a talking point in the media, countless ones get handled with astonishing efficiency. The reality is, those events never come out. They don't come out as nobody wants to be a hero. These great men just believe it's their duty and there is no greater reward for them than their personal satisfaction.

Though it looks like everything is going good for them, sadly, these good times don't last long. They are protected and supported as long as they have a like-minded ecosystem around them. Invariably, the go-getters are the first ones to get targeted once the direction of the winds change unexpectedly. It's just like the evergreen story that we keep hearing—the trees with the sweetest mangoes get targeted first. The trees just have to bear with it and keep giving out mangoes for the benefit of the humankind. But here, it's a different set of challenges that they need to bear. With their proactiveness and zeal, they can take on the high and mighty. With a political change at the seat of power, all of these come back to haunt them, and in no time at all, the affected parties gang up against the officers. Some of these go-getters are shunted to some farthest corners of the state. I remember one of my inspectors was thrown away to a corner of the state, easily some 500 km away, just because he took on somebody who was powerful. He did it because that was his job. It took us almost a year to get him back with letters, angry phone calls and finally, pleading with my superior officers. Their colleagues themselves would also target them because they were an 'inconvenience'.

Again, we all have studied in our moral science classes how the straight tree gets cut first because it makes for excellent windows and frames. With them being surrounded on all sides and often not being too politically aware or shrewd to understand what was hitting them, these officers sometimes become victim to personal issues with their own families as well. This was the saddest thing to see and I tried my best to intervene, sometimes unsuccessfully, as well. It is at times like these that their family, whom they invariably fell back on, are also not in a position to understand their erratic behaviours or mood swings. Just like that, we start losing good officers for no fault of their own as the system has let them down so badly. Still, some choose to stay strong like that mango tree and stand straight as well. It is for all of those men of mettle that we need to stand shoulder to shoulder as they are some very rare gems of the highest quality.

The Ace Investigator

There is a new found interest in the workings of the police in recent times. Much of the general public, who have nothing to do with the daily workings of the police, are keen to know how a case is cracked. This has happened especially after the Over The Top (OTT) platforms like Amazon and Netflix start releasing crime-related series or other series that are based on real crimes. This is an attempt to demystify the crime work the policemen do and the skills that go into cracking cases. Solving crimes is not everybody's cup of tea. Over a point of time, some officers and men develop a flair for it and they become experts at it. They become so good at this that they become full-time crime fighters. They are our faceless heroes. They never come out for media briefings, never have their names out on paper and choose to stay behind the curtains.

A few decades back, crime fighting was altogether a different ball game. Most of the major cases were centred around the occasional murder, highway robberies and dacoities, house theft, cattle theft etc. The society was also fairly homogenised and with urban conglomerates not around, a policeman used to cultivate local spies or informers for him. This was the policeman's first point of contact and these informers would feed him the details of a newcomer in that area—any suspicious conversations with the general public, any travelling gangs or a group of people nearby—and this information was mostly sufficient to pin down the culprits. The policemen in a station also started maintaining a Modus Operandi (MO) sheet which contained the peculiar and unique ways in which crimes had been committed around that area and kept a tab on who committed them. Later, if a criminal became more active, separate criminal sheets were maintained for him. This codified information was useful for the following reason: if a crime with a similar MO was committed in that area, the police would know who the culprit might be. Secondly, this information was needed for the neighbouring police stations as well, as there the culprits could be operating in a bigger geographical area. That's how the initial documentation in the pre-computer era began.

One of the most important discoveries was that of the uniqueness of every single human being's fingerprint and this helped the police in a major way post its adaption into the crime-fighting world. Separate fingerprint bureaus were established at the district and state levels and most of the criminals' fingerprints were collected meticulously whenever he was arrested and stored. Later in any crime scene, a separate trained team started collecting the fingerprints and compared them to the existing database. This was done manually with the help of large lenses and scopes. A separate cadre of policemen became highly specialised by doing this repetitively. Some of them could compare fingerprints by just glancing at them and they became indispensable to the crime work.

The police were able to nab criminals with astonishing regularity and at the police station level, a group of men developed a flair for it—as they tried doing only this. They went beyond catching criminals and started developing a huge intelligence network by understanding the criminals' families better, their weaknesses, their accomplices and receivers (the person who receives the stolen articles from him). Over time, this knowledge became institutional and generations started handing over this repository to the next generation so that the latter could stand on their shoulders and wouldn't have to start from ground zero.

If we look at the society now, it has changed beyond most people's imagination. Cities have become extremely dense and most people don't know who their neighbours are. With technology also leap-frogging with its offerings, the police now are grappling with a new set of challenges. Fingerprints are no longer as useful; the odd person in the group not easily identifiable; and the MOs might not help in a city setting. This is also attributed to a fact that criminals are fast learners and their whole lives are dependent on not getting caught. They will do everything in their power to evade the police.

The best place for them to learn would be the jails, which have become incubators of new crime or act as universities for them to learn from the best. That's why, of late, we see some of the major crimes being planned from within the walls of the prisons. There are also cases where the main accused, who is most often the conspirator, will be inside the jail throughout the whole operation making it all the more difficult to pin him down. Some of the major criminals, by working hand in glove with a local policeman, activates one of the pending warrants against him and enters the jail at a time convenient to him. This then becomes his alibi. Only after he is locked up does he engage in the remote elimination of a rival (usually through *supari* killing). With the advent of smart technologies, several criminals also understand how to use it for crimes like a call spoofing, using tools that might not pin his location to a particular area, call routing and using the dark web to make payments with bitcoins.

There are endless possibilities that technology offers—it provides them a safe hideout in the digital world. Also, with criminals travelling faster between locations, it's impossible to act fast and zero-in on the accused. There are examples where a criminal flies down from a northern Indian state to Bangalore, commits a house theft and coolly escapes in a matter of hours to his place. With the world becoming more interconnected, the police have to be a step ahead of all these factors, especially the criminals. Here we have our 'ace investigators', who are our go-to men, who are willing to go to any length in order to bring the culprits to justice.

An ace investigator, as I have seen, can be anyone, even the lowest-ranked member of the team. He could be a junior constable—what matters is whether he has got a flair for the crime work. This flair is developed and sandpapered over a lifetime. He remains inconspicuous in a room and most often has one of the meekest of voices. These are the people who have taught me whatever little I know of crime fighting. They are the people who, when the entirety of the top leadership is under tremendous pressure after a sensational crime, save us by zeroing-in on the culprit. They have solved some of India's toughest crimes and they are the ones who keep the notorious criminals under check.

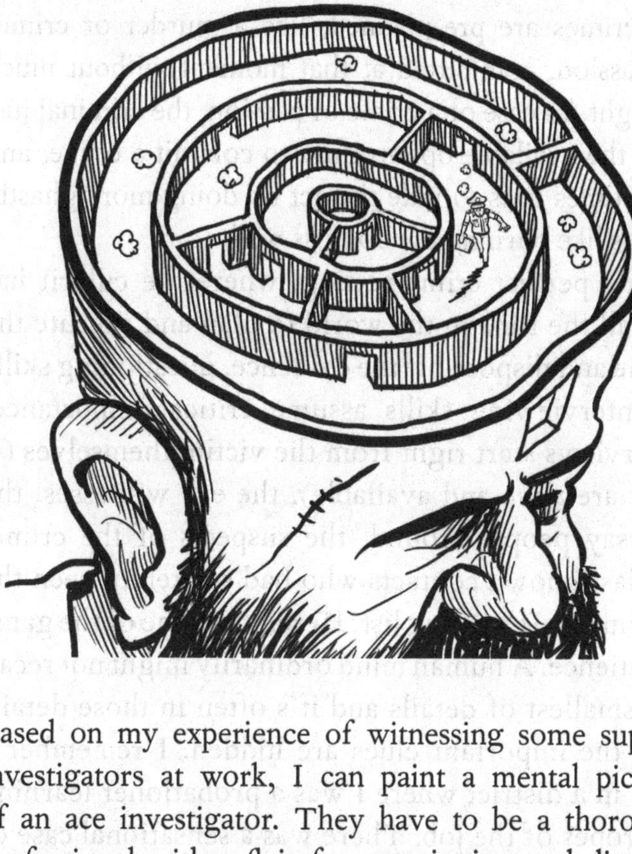

Based on my experience of witnessing some superb investigators at work, I can paint a mental picture of an ace investigator. They have to be a thorough professional with a flair for questioning and digging the truth out. They also need to have a good sense of intuition that is honed over years of hard work. That's why some of our seasoned ones are the more senior ones and are in much demand for many of the complex cases. It goes without saying that hard work and the ability to see the big picture are the ones that more often than not combine with the other necessary traits to get the job done.

As they say, there is nothing called a perfect crime and the criminal always leaves a clue or there's a tell tale story in the way the crime is committed. Some of the crimes are pre-planned, like a murder or crimes of passion, committed at that moment without much thought. In case of a crime of passion, the criminal just uses the available opportunity to commit a crime, and sometimes tries to hide the act by doing more ghastly things like burning the body as well.

In a perfect crime setting, where the culprit has had all the time in the world to plan and execute the crime and dispose off the evidence, questioning skills or interviewing skills assume critical importance. Interviews start right from the victim themselves (if they are alive and available), the eye witnesses, the hearsay people around, the suspects of the crime, the last known contacts who had spoken or seen the victim etc. It's a long list. Here, the name of the game is patience. A human mind ordinarily might not recall the smallest of details and it's often in those details that the important clues are hidden. I remember a case in a district where I was a probationer learning the ropes of the job. There was a sensational case of dacoity in a house and I went to the house multiple times with a crime constable to talk to the victims. The constable used to ask questions to the family very patiently right down to the smallest detail. He would rewind the whole scene minute by minute and help the victims to recall any tiny bit. It could be the colour of the dacoits' clothes, their smell, what they were doing inside the house, the conversation among the dacoits, etc.

The victims, in shock for the initial few days, cooperated to the best of their abilities. They would answer all the questions patiently. The victims were also gaged during the time of dacoity and severely beaten. There was also a young boy of eleven amongst them who was beaten too and he was severely traumatised. Finally, on the thirteenth day, the boy was able to suddenly recall a conversation by the accused with startling accuracy. He said one dacoit had mentioned the power outage 'yesterday' to his accomplice. This is when there was a power cut for a couple of minutes, in the middle of the dacoity. This was enough for our constable to work things backwards and realise that the criminals were present the day before in the same locality as well. He guessed they would have recced the spot of the crime and during further enquiry we found a neighbouring state car roaming around a day before the crime. On the day of the crime, they came by bikes for easy movement with the booty. It was magic to see the way our guy was able to work it out, trace the car to a lodge in the nearby city and crack this case in quick time. This being my first exposure to a major case, I can vividly remember that moment when the boy opened up. It was pure magic.

Human behaviour and the human psyche are important but often neglected parts of crime fighting. A trained crime fighter, by virtue of talking to a huge number of people in his career, understands the psyche of human beings quite well. He can give psychologists a run for their money in his understanding of human behaviour. He can easily point out who is lying and who is hiding information most times. It's also a common occurrence that the person known to the victim would be the culprit—this is most often the case with child molestation or rape and murder, where the violators misuse their familiarity with the victim. They pose as sufferer during the cremation, and in the initial days after the crime, support the family emotionally. Just by observing them carefully, a trained crime fighter would be able to pick out the suspicious signals which their body emits. This is possible by paying very close attention to the person in question and knowing what to pick up from somebody. Sometimes, when one of the accused is caught and the race is on for catching the others, this human behaviour plays an important role. In order to break down the accused, it is important to identify his or her sensitive points. This is an art—the art of making somebody open up. Gone are the days of merciless beating and other third-degree torture techniques. A good understanding of human behaviour will often be the critical link between the criminal and the crime. Eye movements, the way people cry, their body language when they are answering an uncomfortable question, the way they contort their bodies when they defend a lie are all pointers that can be picked up only by a trained eye and an eye that has seen thousands of human beings in that setting.

Malcolm Gladwell, in his book, *Blink: The Power of Thinking Without Thinking,* talks about the concept of making expert judgements. He explains how mental processes work rapidly and automatically with relatively less information. He also extensively speaks about how prejudices and biases affect this snap judgement, but gives a clear primer to what is called 'intuition'. We call this 'gut feeling', but as we all know, guts can't think. So, it's mostly a case of the subconscious brain in operation here. This feeling is akin to a firefighter being able to tell just when a building will collapse. If you ask the fireman later, how did he know when the building would fall, you'll probably get a reply on the lines of 'I just felt it'.

This power of making snap expert judgments comes to somebody who has spent enough time in a particular field. All a firefighter has to do is sense the heat in the air and in the ground and compare that rapidly with what has happened previously in other similar situations. The sense organs work overtime in high-stakes situations to pick up even the littlest of things. I have seen similar instances with good investigators, who have that keen sense of intuition. They are accurately capable of saying, so and so is the culprit, or in some cases, they have an idea about the path to pursue. It is definitely not an 'Aha!' moment; this moment is hard-earned through a lifetime of dedication to their craft. In the initial phase of my career, I was stunned to see our crime constables predicting who the culprits could be. Later, with the progression of time and by gaining that valuable experience, I was able to appreciate it when they told me this. More often than not, without any question, I would trust them and pour resources on their leads.

All said and done, there is no substitute for hard work. Most of the critical cases are ones where the policemen are racing against time. There will be public outcry, media scrutiny, opposition parties putting the ruling party (and thereby the government) on the mat, etc.

With all cases becoming sensational once the media steps in, policemen have to work non-stop to curb any rumours from self-actualising. Serious law and order issues also crop up after communal murders and other serious crimes. I remember in the case of a minor girl's rape and murder, we had to work continuously for three days without a break. With seventeen teams operating at different locations in four districts and feeding us crucial information, it became all the more important to instantaneously react to all the information, decipher the data that was coming in and identify new leads that had to be pursued, so that the teams could then pursue them and the old ones discarded. Time was of essence—the core team was operating at full throttle without any questions of a break. I remember while working on that case, my colleagues would take a few hours' nap by rotation, and work for straight twenty hours every day. A minute or a day that gets wasted is the extra minute or the day the culprit gets to escape from us.

I have also seen some cases where the crime team goes at full speed for almost a month with the same intensity. Though they get back to their routine lifestyles after a couple of days to focus on daily law and order or the general administration, they are relentless and keep up the same energy till they crack the case. Having the ability to work hard is a priceless one and sadly, it is a fast disappearing trait now.

An ace investigator must also be able to quickly solve puzzles. Nobody at a crime scene or in the police investigation can work in a silo. It is true that there could be a first among equals. There could be technical teams, field teams and the team that sits behind and does all the interrogation. There could also be teams that work equally hard on some other things like checking with sources and informants or being present at the crime scene. If an investigator can't analyse all these little bits, they will invariably miss the big picture. These small teams are all pieces of the puzzle. By fitting pieces of the puzzle, through patient listening and being open to the fact that there may be blind spots in his investigation, the ace investigator is able to crack the case. On several occasions, I have seen simple RTA investigations point to a murder. What seems a mere accident at first later turns out to be a larger conspiracy of a string of planned murders waiting to happen.

The traits that are described here are only the most critical ones. They, by no means, cover all the other necessary attributes that are also important in an investigator. Some might have a few and some others. When they combine to form a team and are willing to collaborate, they become deadly. Things like being a team player with a good attitude, an advanced understanding of technology and a passion to serve the public are all critical attributes as well.

The Criminal for You

Who is a criminal? Everyone seems interested in the answer to this for their own reasons; for the policemen to do better at their jobs, criminologists for research purposes, or even plain curiosity for others. Over the years, several of these people have asked me about this. Here, I have tried my best to answer those questions. Who, indeed, is a criminal?

Any person who commits an act that is not sanctioned by the society's mores is called a deviant. These deviants are known to violate the norms and laws of society. Classification becomes difficult; after all, even Gandhi and Mandela were deemed criminals at one point. Nelson Mandela was even incarcerated for twenty-seen years! But somebody's law, even if it's legally ratified, could be seen by another group as illegal and they might choose not to abide by it. Like Mahatma Gandhi, when deciding to disobey the 'lawful' authority in Bihar's Champaran district in 1917, when he took on the cause of the indigo cultivators. This was the first of many by him. We have to be a little careful with respect to categorising someone as 'criminal' for violating a man-made law. Here, we will look at criminal who violates universal laws that are accepted by almost all countries and codified into their statute books as crime.

There is already a very interesting body of work that is available in the field of criminology. Whether criminals are born or created is an age-old question with people vociferously championing both sides. In short, the argument is about whether there is a criminal gene in our body or a criminal is a creature of their circumstances. In this nature vs nurture argument, an army doctor from Italy in the early nineteenth century, Cesare Lombroso, took the early lead for the nature side. His book, *Criminal Man*, written in 1876 argued for physical characteristics determining whether someone will be a criminal or not.[1]

He went on to say criminals were born and could be distinguished by their facial features. To quote from his book, 'At the sight of that skull, I seemed to see all of a sudden...the problem of the nature of the criminal—an atavistic being who reproduces in his person the ferocious instincts of primitive humanity and the inferior animals'.[2] He was refereeing to the indentation at the back of a dead criminal's skull. 'Thus were explained anatomically the enormous jaws, high cheek bones found in criminals, savages and apes.'[3] Further, he argued, 'love of orgies and the irresistible craving for evil for its own sake, the desire not only to extinguish life in the victim, but to mutilate the corpse, tear its flesh, and drink its blood'.[4] In fact, Lombroso went as far as to create a workshop in which he started to experiment with different parts of the human anatomy, especially the skulls. He called this 'The Museum of

[1] Becky Little. 'What Type of Criminal Are You? 19th-Century Doctors Claimed to Know by Your Face', *History*, 8 August 2019. https://www.history.com/news/born-criminal-theory-criminology

[2] Ibid

[3] Ibid

[4] Ibid

Criminal Anthropology' and this was opened to the public from 2009 in Turin, Italy. For a time, he was considered an authority on this subject and used to help enforcement agencies to identify criminals only by studying their physical appearances.

Later, Francis Galton, a British anthropologist, experimented with 'eugenics' and there were also studies done by the Harvard University anthropologist, Earnest A Hooton, on close to 17,000 people in the 1930s to reaffirm Lombroso's arguments.

Over time, almost all of these theories were debunked by later criminologists as stereotypical and racist. At least in our system, this approach is not used now but our country had a very sordid saga of following a particular form of Lombroso's teachings during the British era.

During British rule in India, starting from the 1870s, entire communities were criminalised and labelled 'Habitual Criminals'. In the Act, they defined this category of criminals as 'addicted to the systematic commission of non-bailable offences'. Once defined by this act, severe restrictions were placed on the movement of the adult male members of the family and they were expected to report and put down signatures weekly at the local police station. The Criminal Tribes Act, enacted in 1871, was applied mostly to the northern parts of India and later was extended to the Bengal Presidency. In 1911, it was also extended to the Madras Presidency. The Criminal Tribes Act 1924 covered pretty much the whole of India. By the time India got its independence in 1947, 1.3 crore people belonging to 127 communities, were covered under this ambit.

With a lot of public outcry, independent India abolished this Act in 1949 and former 'criminal tribes' were denotified in 1952. They were reclassified into 313 nomadic tribes and 198 denotified tribes in India. That is close to six crore people. In 1952, independent India also enacted the Habitual Offenders Act where the offender was described as 'manifesting a set practice in crime'. The British, brought under their Act entire castes, occupations, tribes and communities like the Thuggees, who were giving them a lot of trouble. Independent India chose to go by the objective criteria of the crimes committed by a person, irrespective of where and to which family he was born.[5]

Criminals, to a major extent, reflect the sociological and economic times of society's evolution. At a certain time in India's history, brewing illicit liquor was classified as a major crime as it was not sanctioned by the state. This was because the state was losing its precious revenue when somebody sold liquor by brewing their own composition illegally. During the time of India's strict import policies, many gangs reared their heads, smuggling gold and other commodities for which there was a market. Major cities had gangs taking control of large areas like the cocaine mafia across major American cities, and were operating those like their personal fiefdoms. Major crimes happened only on the issue of who controlled what. With the era of liberalisation in India, unused land inside the city became pots of gold

[5] Sanjay Nigam. "Disciplining and Policing the 'criminals by birth', Part 1: The Making of a colonial stereotype – The criminal tribes and castes of North India". *Indian Economic & Social History Review*.1990. 27 (2): 131–164.

and various groups, including the infamous Mumbai mafias, were born. Later, they expanded their operations to get into all sorts of criminal activities.

So many criminals are born due to circumstances and they are propelled by greed to commit all the acts they are committing. The criminals that we have discussed here are the big ones, who sometimes kept changing their avatars as well. Many get into legal businesses to change the course of their lives, some very daringly enter the field of education and many into politics as well. Since their tracks are very well hidden, we often don't know about their sketchy pasts. They often pose as our next-door neighbours and we are none the wiser.

The other sets of criminals are the daily criminals who keep coming across the police radar. Because they were so regular, they were classified as 'habitual offenders', as defined under the Habitual Offenders Act of 1952. This is the category where I got to see many interesting people during my career. They were the usual house burglars, chain snatchers, commercial shop lifters, etc. This kind is so prone to committing crimes that their whole world revolves around this ecosystem. The kind of people they meet, their associates—including their lawyers—are all part of this environment. They cannot live a life that is anything other than that of crime. Most of them got into the world of crime through their family members or through their 'gurus'. The other problem is crossing that threshold age after which picking up employable skills becomes a problem. So they stick on to their world of crimes. The cobwebs are so strong that even if they want to leave this life of crime, they would not able to.

I once had an interesting conversation with a 'Habitual Offender' to understand why it was so tough to come out of this life of crime with all its risks and the continuous fear of police. His answers to my questions were illuminating and he ended up unwittingly teaching me one or two lessons about psychology.

By then, the criminal to whom I was talking to had got about seventeen cases against him. He had gone to jail multiple times and he was out on a court bail at the time. With warrants being issued against him in nine cases, he had to make a regular habit of visiting the courts or else he would attract their wrath. His monthly expenditure bill for the lawyers alone was coming to be about ₹40,000 and he was heavily indebted to his lawyer for bailing him out in all of those cases. I could understand from him that his lawyers are also dependent on him like he is dependent on the lawyer.

In this vicious cycle, the same criminal justice system which was supposed to reform him, was actually suffocating him and not allowing him to come out of a life of crime. The moot point was this—where would he find a job? So he had got into an understanding with the local policemen that he would not commit crimes within their territories but he would do so in other jurisdictions. For that, he wanted the policemen to give him some sort of protection when other station personnel came hunting for him. In return, he was willing to offer some sort of intelligence about crimes happening in their jurisdiction. I knew for a fact that these kinds of delicate arrangements were being maintained across the station jurisdictions for all local criminals. The more proficient a criminal was, the more entrenched these kinds of arrangements became into the police system.

On the other hand, we have some very interesting criminal gangs that are in operation across our country now. Some of these gangs got birthed post the abolition of the Criminal Tribes nomenclature in 1949. Their world is completely separate from ours and they operate in total secrecy pan-India like a well-oiled machine.

One of the gangs over the years that has gained notoriety and respect is the famous (or infamous) Ramji Nagar gang from Tiruchirappalli, Tamil Nadu.

'The residents of Ramji Nagar belong to a particular community from Andhra Pradesh, who migrated during the pre-independence era and settled in Thogamalai in Karur, the then combined Tiruchy district. In Tiruchy, they are called 'kepmari', but there is no clear explanation or proof of how they got the name. But, in those days, they were ex-communicated in most places by the village heads after repeated complaints of theft against them. Later, in order to rehabilitate the habitual offenders, the then district administration created a settlement for them near Ramji Moolji Cotton Mill in 1936 in Trichy (the present Ramji Nagar) and offered them jobs. However, a section continued to involve in stealing and gradually started to try their hands in other states. Now there are over 1500 families with at least two in a family sticking to the 'ancestral profession.'[6]

6 *DTNEXT*. 'Can Ramji Nagar clean its stain?' *DTNEXT*, 3 October 2016. https://www.dtnext.in/News/City/2016/10/03012856/Can-Ramji-Nagar-clean-its-stain.vpf

This gang, comprising a whole village, is India's leading attention-diversion gang (where the attention of the gullible victim is diverted and money or any other valuable is stolen) and they operate across Bangalore, Hyderabad, Mumbai, Delhi, Calcutta and other financial centres like Ahmedabad. I have come across this gang a couple of times and tried to, unsuccessfully, catch them. It is always a case of one or two getting caught, mostly the lower-ranking members, but never the honchos. I'll illustrate a typical case and this might give a better idea about this gang's operations. This gang normally operates around a bank, insurance office, post office or other financial entities, where the victim is likely to draw some money and come out. The first and the foremost thing, their leader—called 'Captain'—has to do, is to pick the right victim, who is older and looks gullible.

Older couples are their preferred choice. When they come out of the above-mentioned centres and take their car or their bikes, one gang member clearly notes down the place where the money is kept, normally on the dashboard, front seat or below the seat. One or two gang members then follow them and here, they adopt different strategies to divert their attention. They either puncture the victims' tyres—they are experts in this and they know exactly to what distance the vehicle can travel—which is a preferred method when dealing with a four-wheeler. In case of a two-wheeler, it could be sprinkling some paint on the shirt and telling the victims to check it out.

When they get off their bikes to wash the paint, one person expertly steals the money bag. Another common option is to throw a ₹50 or ₹100 rupee note on the ground and asking the driver to check if it's theirs. The human tendency of getting down and picking it up is enough for them to reach in and take the bundle of cash out. They operate with extreme finesse thanks to their rigorous training. Boys as young as twelve are brought into the trade and by virtue of their training, they become experts by sixteen. The team leader uses hand signals to direct, lead and also to escape. They try their best not to harm any victim, as they know this unwanted attention will make the police come after them. Once the booty is taken out, it is shared. A major cut goes to the 'Captain' and a contribution is made to the common fund for the local committee at Ramji Nagar so as to evade arrest and cover other expenses like courts and jails. A certain percentage is also compulsorily donated to the local deity. The remaining amount is shared among the gang members. With no police cooperation in Tamil Nadu (as the gang doesn't function there anymore), other state police personnel find it impossible to penetrate into this area as the ladies surround the police teams and shield their adult males. They go even to the extent of filing molestation complaints against the visiting policemen. Their connections with local politicians and movers and shakers of that area are also well-oiled. They believe in pujas and omens before starting for a crime across the country and depend on the Tamil *panchangam* (almanac) to decide the time and direction of their venture. The Ramji Nagar gang, for almost all the police teams across India, remains a mystery. In the northern part of India, they are called 'Tak Tak' gangs because of the sound of their knock in the glass windows of a car.[7]

[7] *The Times of India*. 'Crorepati thief brought from Trichy in handcuffs', *The Times of India*, 15 November 2014. https://timesofindia.indiatimes.com/city/ahmedabad/Crorepati-thief-brought-from-Trichy-in-handcuffs/articleshow/45154549.cms

There are other notorious gangs like the OG Kuppam gang in the Chittoor district of Andhra Pradesh. They follow almost the same MO as the Ramji Nagar gang but they also take recourse to itching sprays. When they spray this on a victim who is riding on a bike, the sensation of itching leads the victim to stop his or her bike. One of the gang members then helps the potential victim by offering him or her water to drink and to wash off the itching sensation. In the meantime, the other gang members expertly disappear with the cash. They mostly operate within their own state, and occassionally in Bangalore as well.

The other gang from the northern India that was made famous by a recent Tamil movie on their MO and operations is the notorious Bawaria gang. These gang members prey on the houses on the highways, brutally assault or even murder their victims and escape with the loot. Their gang was in news regarding the recent Bulandshar rape case. Bawarias are a nomadic tribe involved in a range of criminal activities for decades now. They primarily operate across Uttar Pradesh but their sightings are also reported from Haryana and Rajasthan—where they originate. Bawariyas are the worst of the 13 nomadic tribes involved in criminal activities in Uttar Pradesh and have operated since pre-Independence times. If challenged, Bawariyas don't hesitate to kill their victims too.[8]

[8] Vishakha Saxena. 'Ruthless, organised and disgusting: All about the Bawariya gang behind Bulandshahr gangrape', *India Today*, 1 August 2016. https://www.indiatoday.in/india/story/bulandshahr-gang-rape-bawariya-gang-332684-2016-08-01

Yet another notorious gang that I have come across during my policing life is the daring and ill-tempered, Indian-Irani gang. They are more notorious in southern India for their chain-snatching and bike-lifting and, in some parts of northern India, for their attention diversion crimes.

'Ambivli, 60 km from Mumbai, is home to the Indian-Irani tribe. Their ancestors were brought from Persia by Golconda's kings who appointed them as bodyguards due to their strong physique and tales of bravery. The nomadic community initially used to live near railway stations and bus depots. Now, they have settlements in Maharashtra, Karnataka, Andhra Pradesh and MP. Iranipada, the slums adjoining Ambivli station, is a major hub of the gang. "Irani gang" members use their good looks to target and loot valuables from the elderly, women, bank customers and poor people.'[9]

They are well-built, muscular and have chiselled looks. They sometimes travel upto 1,000 km without a break, committing various offences along the way. When police personnel enter their area for any kind of investigation, they are treated with total impunity without any fear of law. As in the words of a police officer, 'There are over 1,000 homes in Iranipada. Several raids and combing operations have been carried out by the police in Mumbai and Thane but most of them are unsuccessful. It is sometimes dangerous to go to their area. They gherao us from all sides and start

[9] Arvind Ojha. 'Thugs of Iran strike fear in Delhi's heart', *India Today*, 10 January 2019. https://www.indiatoday.in/mail-today/story/thugs-of-iran-strike-fear-in-delhis-heart-1427526-2019-01-10

pelting stones at us. There is very little support from the local police who don't enter their area at all.'

In cases of sexual assaults and paedophilia, I have seen that most of the culprits are the people known to the victims, like their neighbours or close relatives. They thoroughly misuse the trust that is placed on them and commit this barbaric act. Most often, they are first-time offenders and initially, I really didn't have a clue as to why they did this horrific act even on a three-year-old child. The available literature is also very sketchy in this regard. Sometimes I fear that Lombroso's predictions might be true but perhaps in a different context, such as the recent research study conducted by a couple of professors in Sweden.[10] In their study, as quoted by *The Guardian*, they were able to link genetic factors as a major cause along with unique environmental factors as a minor cause for the depredation in their mindset:

> The scientists used the records of 21,566 men convicted of sexual offences in Sweden between 1973 and 2009. Around 2.5% of brothers or fathers of convicted sex offenders were themselves convicted of sexual offences, compared to an offending rate of about 0.5% of men in the general population. The authors looked at both rape and child sexual offences and found similar patterns for both. About 40% of sexual offending risk is explained by genetic

[10] Niklas Långström, Kelly M Babchishin, Seena Fazel, Paul Lichtenstein, Thomas Frisell. 'Sexual offending runs in families: A 37-year nationwide study', *International Journal of Epidemiology*, Volume 44 (2): 713–720, 2 April 2015. https://academic.oup.com/ije/article/44/2/713/753089?sid=54782729-3119-463f-acff-0ed9c7662bff

> factors, a statistical analysis found, and about 2% of the risk was attributed to environmental factors shared between siblings, such as parental attitudes, neighbourhood and education. The risk was found to be slightly higher for brothers (five times the average) compared to fathers (four times), which could simply reflect brothers being closer in age and therefore more likely to both offend during the study period. Unique environmental factors, such as head injuries, peer group influence and social experiences, are likely to account for the remaining differences in risk between people.[11]

To understand any crime in its true perspective, the psychology of criminals needs to be studied, something that is sadly not happening. During my interrogation of some of these sexual predators, I found their sense of morality and sense of right and wrong very skewed and no amount of hard punishments might reform them. We can throw a thousand criminals in jail and many can be hanged but if we don't do a professional study on the criminals—especially the sexual predators and paedophiles—we will never be able to solve these crimes enough.

[11] Hannah Devlin. 'Risk of sex offending linked to genetic factors, study finds', *The Guardian*, 9 April 2015. https://www.theguardian.com/science/2015/apr/09/risk-of-sex-offending-linked-to-genetic-factors-study-finds

The Night Watchman Called Khaki

This is more about the story of our policemen in totality. Who are they and why do they do what they do? In short, this is the story of their life, their hope and their aspirations, their tragedies, the reason they become policemen at all. A policeman is most often misunderstood. Even I needed a few years of policing experience to see the reality with full objectivity. The policeman is still the powerful villain in the movie and the hero is shown as brave, taking on a mighty villain. It's common to hear conversations like this, 'Hey, if you don't eat, I will call that police uncle. He will take you away.' The image that gets fed to us, reinforces a powerful belief—that a policeman will be called to discipline us. These and many other stereotypes keep reinforcing the artificial narrative around the khaki and that's why most of our men are still looked down on as night watchmen by the common public.

Let's rewind a couple of centuries back to see how it started. The East India Company (EIC), which was granted a trading license by the Mughals, later got ambitious and went to the extent of grabbing territories. It raised a local sepoy troop in Calcutta and Madras to fight off their regional rivals and finally to take on the Mughals themselves. By the time Lord Cornwallis took over as the Governor General of India (1786–1793), the EIC was ruling most of extended India. For effective administration, they created a semblance of a police force under the District Judge. Each district was divided into *thanas* or police circles, each of which was for approximately 20 square miles. It was placed under an Indian officer, called the *daroga*, who was ably assisted by many constables.

However, the police organisation was not effective and in the words of John Clark Marshman (1794-1877), an English missionary and who set up the first newspaper in Bengali language,[1] 'The *daroga* enjoyed almost unlimited power of extortion and became the scourge of the country'. After the British crown took over Indian affairs, the Police Act of 1861 was brought in. The Indian Imperial Police was raised under Section 5 of the Act and had both the superior police services and the subordinate police services. By 1905, the Imperial Police became part of the Indian Police Services. After independence, and in keeping with the federal character of the constitution of India, the drafters of the constitution granted both the public order and police to the states (these are the first two entries in the State List).

There was also a provision made for entry 2A in the Union List (Deployment of any armed force of the Union or any other force subject to the control of the Union or any contingent or unit thereof in any state in aid of the civil power; powers, jurisdiction, privileges and liabilities of the members of such forces

[1] John Clark Marshman. *The Darogah's Manual, Comprising also the Duties of Landholders in Connection with the Police*, 1850.

while on such deployment), but this was purely to aid any state during a time of need. There is an IPS cadre that is exclusively recruited by the centre through an independent agency—the UPSC—and given to the states for the maintenance of their police forces. This complex arrangement, with most states having their own kind of state police force was, in a way, made to preserve the federal nature of our republic and to give the states the independence and freedom that they deserved. As an unintending side effect, this is one of the reasons why the police forces in each state are at differing levels of growth and efficiency. Being at the mercy of states, and with various states evolving at their own speed, policemen were made a tool not of the state but of the political masters who run a state.

I had, for some time, seen and believed that a country like India continued to thrive on three contradicting facets—eighteenth century laws, nineteenth century mindset and twenty-first century aspirations. Inside this maze is where our policemen reside. A police force that once attracted the best of its citizens is no more able to do so. Any organisation has to progressively get attractive and keep up with the aspirations of GenZ. Only then it will start growing in its stature and attract the best to come in and be a part of it. It also has to be in tune with growth of the country and the opportunities that have exploded in other spheres. With most of the government service recruitments not happening on a regular basis, and the police being one of the major recruiting forces, we see in all our recruitments a common phenomenon—thousands of people participating.

The recruitment for the constabulary attracts a ratio of 1:150 (posts to applicants) in different recruitment cycles and people from all kinds of backgrounds apply as the entry threshold is kept very low—having appeared for class X final exams. I have seen PhD candidates applying as well, but this job is definitely not designed for them. Not only is the work very demanding and draining, but the pay is also quite less. We would be deluding ourselves if we assume we can convince them and sell the idea of 'service' to them. They see it as a job with prestige, and I can say with certainty that nobody at the entry-level in policing is attracted by the idea of service.

For them, the prestige of joining a government profession, especially if they're from the rural and semi-rural background, is very attractive. This is the pull that brings them to a district headquarter to pass the fitness and written tests. This can be sustained only till the initial sheen wears off. With over-qualified candidates getting selected (often people with an undergraduate degree and sometimes even more), once they come in and after their training is over, they try their best to get out of the service. Here, the very famous psychological theory of cognitive dissonance is in operation. People with dissonance will prepare and appear for other competitive exams like those for Panchayat Development Officers, teachers and so on, but these not being very regular recruitments, they wear their uniform with two minds. Many of the younger constables keep looking over their shoulders for other career prospects. This creates a very heavy attrition and sometimes these attrition numbers are very close to twenty per cent of the selected batches for Police Constables (PCs). In case of armed reserve police forces, the attrition rate is at an enormous high, over thirty per cent and topping at fifty per cent for some batches.[2] Often, I used to try and find answers by talking to the young constables who would come and meet me with their resignation papers. My only job was to try and find out whether they were quitting with a sense of better possibilities being available to them or out of disgust. I tried and counselled them only if it were the latter. Invariably, many of them gave the same answer to me (more like an exit interview) on why they wanted to quit—the culture.

The culture in the police force can be indirectly compared to the pernicious caste culture that has taken hold of our country, though not literally but figuratively. Though I strongly disapprove of this classification and keep fighting it out, this unfortunately is the reality that still exists. The various entry levels in the Indian police force, unlike in other western democracies, creates an artificial barrier and adversely affects the culture. An IPS officer who comes in at the senior level is akin to a Brahmin sitting at the top of the hierarchy—the all-powerful and all-knowing; the second level of the Deputy Superintendents and Police Sub-Inspectors (typically, recruited by the state governments as per their constitutional right) are the Kshatriyas and Vaishyas—the resourceful and controlling. The constabulary, who are the bottom

[2] Data from the office of ADGP, Recruitment and Training, Bengaluru.

rung and includes Constables, Head Constables and Assistant Sub-Inspectors, are the Shudras—the serving ones who are bereft of any dignity. If we analyse each of them, we will realise that they come from certain socio-economic spheres of life and this rift has kept getting deeper over the years. Some countries, most notably Britain, which has introduced the multiple recruitment models to our country, have only a single-entry system. So everybody joins as a constable and keeps moving upwards in service. That's why the police commissioner of London is called the Chief Constable. They want to fine-tune this further by improving the quality of their recruitments and a major change is due in 2020–2021.

So naturally the ranks tend to congregate among themselves. Some good officer might come and emphasise the esprit de corps once in a while but exceptions never make examples. This is the biggest challenge facing our forces now. With deep divisions among the ranks, the workload unevenly distributed and meritocracy not given any importance, the police as an organisation is slowly dying. The standards of the incoming batches are good with respect to technology usage but not so great on grounds of the empathy that needs to be shown. Also, the institutional authority for which the police was famed is also slowly eroding. There were times when the sub-inspectors' writ ran large in their areas and now we have reduced them to a mere symbol.

In the last few decades, with the political sphere seeing a severe degradation in its values, the ruling politicians have quickly learnt a valuable lesson—without police power, political power is as good as useless. This is most applicable to the grassroots politicians, who are at the dust bowl of Indian democracy. The inspectors and the sub-inspectors get posted to particular areas through an understanding with the local MLAs of the ruling government in that place. This is an important arrangement that keeps the local politicians happy and allows the party apparatus to remain self-sustaining. In some states like Karnataka, this practice is even institutionalised in the form of a 'minute system'[3] where the ruling political executive, in his official letter pad, writes to the government about who the officer posted there should be. With the senior police leadership literally obeying all of these orders in toto, the police officials at the local station and circle levels have become thoroughly politicised. Many a times, it is alleged that money is exchanged for this and apparently these transactions easily run into multiple lakhs.

The officers who get posted are very clear where their loyalties lie and the higher officers of the IPS ranks who are supposed to keep a check on the moral fabric of the policing culture invariably stand as mute spectators, barring a few. These few get shunted for their 'impractical mindset' and the rest become active collaborators to benefit from this in the long run as many sought-after posts are available for the 'right person'. With the major political leaders publicly identifying themselves more with their caste of birth than with their track record as a leader, castes have also become a

[3] Raghunandan PM. 'Transfer racket: Officials pay in lakhs for plum posts', *Deccan Herald*, 5 September 2018. https://www.deccanherald.com/special-features/transfer-racket-officials-pay-690630.html

major factor along with money power now. Invariably, the castes which were shunted out during the previous governments, make a comeback once their leaders are back to ruling the roost. For this class of officers, now is the time to make good of what was lost.

This cycle of money, combined with caste, has corrupted the soul of the whole police force and it is in this culture that constabulary is expected to keep serving the public without any reward; not even a fair salary or the tools of the trade that might make it an equal fight for them. Since these grievances are not effectively articulated and therefore, not addressed, sometimes they think of the unthinkable. For instance, in Karnataka, on 4 June 2018, the constables tried to go on strike. This was effectively squashed by the state by constituting a committee to study their grievances and by the threat of invoking the tough ESMA (Essential Services Maintenance Act) against them. It is in these circumstances that a constable is expected to perform and deliver, apart from also knowing that their bosses sitting at the top are possibly compromised. This creates a scenario where most of the orders of a sub-inspector or inspector are looked upon with suspicion and in some cases, disobeyed. I have had cases in the last few years where files have come to me recommending a constable's suspension on flimsy grounds. When I tried enquiring over this issue, I found out that this 'insubordination' was invariably over the constable's refusal to toe the inspector's bidding. These instances are getting more acute as the new breed of constables are more educated, social-media savvy and are prepared to question their officers' motives in the general roll call (meetings) that happens inside a station. Their grievances are not being met and the pent up frustrations are leading them to so-called indiscipline and groupism on caste or economic lines inside a police station, which is also a serious cause for concern.

Not only are the policemen expected to perform their duty with limited resources but also often, they are denied their most important, legitimate right—their leave. This creates cascading, less-studied, long-term effects on their families. Their absence to perform their duties also as a parent, spouse and child affects adversely the sacred bond within their family. I have seen countless cases where the family of policemen thrive despite him or her, the children grow up very fast and start taking charge of their lives without the 'police parent' having a meaningful contribution to their growth. This is evident, as I have seen on the day's of policemen's retirement where rarely the entire families attend the function. On probing, I have found that their relationships are not very cordial and this is not surprising.

I only feel sorry for the conditions that keep our policemen away from their families. Wherever I was posted, I had a rule that every policeman should take a compulsory weekly off (meaning, he or she should take a day off a week by rotation). Initially, I had the most resistance from the policemen themselves. They were giving all sorts of reason to get back to duty as I had detailed earlier in the book. This, I realised, was the power of habit—a repeated participation in a static culture that bore no rewards. The very same culture has

also made policemen temporarily freeze their thinking as well. They are okay with the substandard food that is given to them during a mass *bandobust* as long as some food is given and a small increase in salary once in a blue moon is fine by them.

This can only change when our attitude towards the police force changes. We will discuss the big vision and the reforms needed in the last chapter for which a political vision and an administrative will is required. The vision and will power might bring in the much needed resources and importance to our men in khaki. What is more important than this is the respect with which the public should treat the policemen. The small attitudinal changes that we as a society need, like respecting a policeman, are sorely lacking. I have seen during my night rounds that some houses offer tea to our night beat staff and some routinely keep a flask of a hot beverage outside. To a guy who is into his fifteenth hour of duty of the day, this will mean a lot. Seeing a cop on the street and not looking at him in derision and instead giving him a polite nod or a smile will do wonders for their morale. Our society, overall, has to bring in the culture where men and women, who serve us despite their ranks, get treated well. I used to joke in police stations with my men that the day the public invites us to an important function in their family, will be the day we can safely assume that our police force is getting closer to the community. Most of our community initiatives are becoming one-way and the necessary support from the public is sorely lacking. This is also in keeping with the overall trend of citizens themselves becoming inward-looking and aloof from the society in which they live. But that is a topic for another day.

Life Lessons from the World of Khaki

The lessons one learns as a policeman, after having seen the workings of our society up close, is priceless. Because of the nature of the law enforcement in India, policemen do all things possible, inside and outside their office. In the morning, he acts as a counsellor to set right a marriage; then, becomes the enforcer of law by day; come evening, he counsels youths addicted to drugs; and in the middle of it all, he regulates traffic or controls a section of a crowd in a *bandobust*. A policeman, especially if he keeps his eyes and ears open, gets the best lesson in human psychology and behaviour. I have gone through most of the emotional highs and lows of being in the thick of action. Some of these are such a high point, I just humbly say a silent prayer to the almighty every time I see those people back in my life. The impression that they leave are so remarkable that I can still recall with clarity the moment I had spent with them. The joy is when I see a husband and wife in a public place very happily moving among the crowds with their child, laughing all the while. I would remember the same couple sitting in my office and bitterly fighting a few years back. I had to reunite them for the sake of their child after close to thirty hours of counselling in a week. The blessing for a cop is when of all the marriages that we must have facilitated when the couples had taken refuge in our office as a last resort, most of them are working well. There are many cases of the couples taking our wishes on their wedding anniversary from far across the world. The moment of total elation for me is when somebody named their child Annamalai just because the couple liked me and appreciated the work I was doing. One gets daily inspiration from knowing with certainty that we have positively touched somebody's life on any given day. All of these have built gratitude, humility and made me realise that it is a blessing to be a police officer.

At the same time, the lows that I had personally experienced were very bitter. When I remember some of those incidents, I can still experience the uncomfortable lurch in my stomach. I can never ever forget a college-going boy dying in a Road Traffic Accident (RTA) and his father crying in my arms outside the mortuary. With his tears on my uniform, I just stood there, not knowing what to do. A five-year-old boy went missing when he was playing outside his house and his parents literally stayed in my office hoping for the best while we conducted our intensive search efforts. Finally, after a few days, we could only find the dismembered body and though the accused was arrested, I can still feel the mother's chilling look in my bones. There have been countless cases where I had to break the news of someone's death to their own parents and had to experience the inevitable moment of silence that captured the space between them and me once I had uttered those fateful words. Some of those were too horrifying, I started to fast for a day in a week to heal my own self. On some days the negative energy would be so high in my body, I would forego a meal just because I couldn't accept an innocent dying for no fault of theirs.

Though I haven't lost any colleague in action under my command, I have lost plenty of them to RTAs and unnatural deaths. A major culprit has been heart attacks, and in some sad instances, suicides as well. At every funeral I attended, my only question would be—if he was not a policeman, would his life have been different? I don't know and I suppose we never know. Seeing some of these intense incidents closely made me seek refuge in spirituality. More than religion, I was trying to understand the energy fields and karma better. I know that it's a hopeless task and I can't crack that code but I kept persisting. This search has taken me to some of the scared places across India, from Kashmir to Kanyakumari. I made a point to travel across the Himalayas for a few years and finally visited Kailash where I took the decision to move out of policing.

When I look back on some of the powerful life lessons for me in my policing career, I can zero down on three of the most important ones.

The training for the All India Service officers (IAS, IPS, IFS) commences with the Foundation Course at the LBSNAA in Mussourie. This ninety-day course is designed to develop the spirit, bonding and most importantly, an officer-like mindset among the probationers. During this period, many eminent officers address us, share their life experiences and lessons.

One such talk was delivered by a former IPS officer who I will only call Raj.[1]

Duing his first posting, Officer Raj was continuously monitoring the movement of a brigand trying to nab him. One day, when he had a near-perfect information on the wanted man's presence at his paramour's house, Officer Raj decided to raid the house and arrest him. A unit consisting of his trusted boys was deployed around the house and across the nearby fields to eliminate the possibility of the brigand sneaking out. A thorough briefing was given to all the policemen about their duties and how are they expected to perform. The plan was to nab the brigand as he arrived at the location. On that fateful day, everything went as planned. The only problem was that the person in question was nowhere to be found. Either he had already reached the house or he was yet to arrive. But the officer trusted his informer and was very sure, the brigand must have reached much ahead of the planned rendezvous time.

In a moment of daring and leadership, Officer Raj decided to barge into the house to take the brigand head-on. He found the house had only one opening, and that too, a not-so strong door. He kept his guards outside, knocked the door down in one blow and rushed into the house, which was basically a small room with a cot and a few utensils. Once inside, he still couldn't find the culprit even though the officer's eyes desperately searched for him. In that moment of confusion, the officer felt the tip of a pistol land behind his head. He

[1] Name changed to protect identity and privacy of the officer.

realised that the brigand was actually near the door when he pushed in.

As Raj considered his options, his mind also raced with fear and his young child's image flashed in front of his eyes. In a desperate effort, he pushed the pistol with his hand and shifted his head all in one go. A ferocious fist-fight broke out between them, with the pistol dangling in the middle. Luckily, the pistol fell out and the officer was on top of this guy in a moment. Raj literally had to chew his way out of the situation, by chewing the brigand's ears and face to finally subdue him.

Later, the officer was sitting outside near the fields and counting on his blessings for being able to escape such a close call. He was also mulling over what could have easily gone wrong—like the brigand firing at him without a moment's thought or him not being lucky in executing that crucial step of taking his head away and pushing the pistol to the side (which in the police academy is mostly taught as a drill, and to implement this in the real world under pressure is a different ball game). It was a very fine line between him emerging as a zero and of a hero. At the same time, an experienced head constable approached him to have a small conversation. The same constable had tried to approach the officer multiple times during the briefing but Raj had to ignore him then due to paucity of time. The head constable said, '*Saab*, don't you think it was downright foolish to barge into that house? You could have been easily killed. This is what I had been trying to tell you during the briefing. The house had only one door and it's too small to be a house with toilets built inside. If at all our guy was inside he had no option but to come out of the house at least to attend nature's call. He couldn't have stayed holed up there for eternity. All we needed was patience, constant vigil and some common sense.'

That was when everything fell in place for Officer Raj. He just stood up, hugged his head constable with tears rolling down his cheeks. This officer went on to be a highly decorated police officer and the winner of the gallantry award at a very young age. He then forayed into politics where he currently has a decorated career as well. With loads of humility and shedding his ego, this officer laid out this lesson to us all, so that we could carry this lesson whenever we wore our khaki. On a parting note he said, 'Common sense is least common, be careful about that as well'.

This was a lesson that had always stayed with me after I had heard it for the first time in 2012. Throughout my service, I had innumerable occasions to plan some action—both big and small. Despite the best of intentions, I tended to over-complicate things and my ego hindered my learning many a times. Finally, with some self-reflection and humility, I have found it's common sense that I had often missed. It was always sobering to be reminded that our minds have most of the answers to our problems but we don't look at them due to our hurry.

A few years into my service, I forced myself to self-reflect daily through compulsive diary-writing. I also got introduced to the spiritual practice of Kriya yoga during the same time and with its daily practice, over the past many years, I'm slowly reaching the zone of conscious inaction. The mind, of course, processes information very fast. Like the famous saying, 'The young are condemned to repeat the mistakes of the old', we too make the same mistakes that were made over the years a thousand times in the same office. With repeated failures initially, I'm now developing this habit of slowing down my decision-making. Leadership is not about action and rushing headlong always, by marching our army. The current world, we believe, tends to reward speed over steadiness, activity over quality, running around over stillness. But is it really so? Or have we assumed the world to be like that?

If we take a proper look, we will realise, it continues to reward steadiness, patience, stillness and through all of this, ultimately, the quality of work. The world hasn't changed much but we have. Millions of people have lived before us on their terms. They have lived purposeful, happy and joyful lives. Somehow, we have confused activity for progress and are riding that non-stop treadmill. Unfortunately, many of us are riding that tiger and neither can we slow it down nor can we climb down when the tiger is in motion. This culture is feeding into lives and changing it for the worse. Technological addiction is one part of that. A possible solution is to change the way we are playing this game and to slow down our life considerably and to get conscious of our existence. However, this is easier said than done.

I have learnt this the hard way. More than knowledge, it is wisdom that makes the eventual difference. That's why even when most of our plans fail, the saying goes 'But still we must plan and fail'. Yes, agreed that planning is an act of preparation and each problem need not be faced with a gavel in hand. The western leadership theories emphasise very heavily on 'action' although deep down it's tough to force ourselves to be in a state of conscious inaction when need arises. Our eastern spiritual literature is abound with this knowledge. To cultivate that state is an arduous task as the natural impulses will always push us to act, and therein lies the problem. We are caught into that vicious cycle.

When closely studying Abraham Lincoln's leadership,[2] what struck me most was the conscious inaction Lincoln displayed when it mattered. History didn't give us full picture about how he slowed down his decision-making process during the Civil War in the 1860s when his whole Cabinet was after him, urging him to act by changing either the General or the strategy of the war.

> 'One of Lincoln's greatest strengths was understanding the power of doing nothing in the heat of the moment. He understood that we rarely make good decisions when emotional temperatures are high and, as a result, he cultivated the self-discipline to take no action in such circumstances.
>
> Consider, for example, the immediate aftermath of the battle of Gettysburg in July 1863, Lincoln was furious that Union General George Meade decided not to pursue the demoralized the Confederate States Army as they headed south—with an eye toward

[2] Nancy Koehen. *Forged in Crises.* John Murray, London, October 2017.

> decisively crushing the enemy once and for all. The president poured his fury into a scathing letter to Meade, writing, "I cannot adequately express my disappointment in this situation." He signed it and put it in an envelope—but he never sent it (The letter was discovered in Lincoln's desk after his death.) By doing nothing, Lincoln made a conscious decision to not risk alienating the Northern general and thus potentially sabotaging his mission to save the Union. Expressing white-hot emotions in the moment, as Lincoln realized, often wreaks damage to the world, your followers, and a noble cause. By contrast, sitting with your emotions and resisting the temptation to act on them does no harm (and, in some cases, may even give the issue at hand the time and space to sort itself out). The power of doing nothing is especially important in our age of instant (and often incendiary) communication on social media.'[3]

One of the greatest of presidents of the USA, fighting a grave crises in the nation's history, didn't allow his impulses to override him. Not only do the important moments but even some simple moments need inaction. We need not always be hypercharged and crave for action. This is a powerful lesson I learnt in the fag end of my policing career and which I'm trying to inculcate in my everyday life.

[3] Nancy Koehn. 'How to lead like Abraham Lincoln, according to a Harvard historian', *Quartz at Work*, 30 July 2018. https://qz.com/work/1343648/how-to-lead-like-abraham-lincoln-according-to-a-harvard-historian/

As a policeman, I have seen too many deaths very closely. I was told by my officers that after a point of time, death numbs you and you are no longer hit by the deaths as much. But every single time I saw a dead body, I always got the same feeling that I had had the first time I saw a body up-close. For most of us, it's during the training at Hyderabad, where we were taken to government hospitals for practical training. To see a disfigured human body lying in the mortuary without any care in the world, is probably the first time I saw most of my group members vomiting. Gone were the names of the human beings that identified them when they were alive. They had only some case numbers or some random digits scribbled on their bodies, which accompanied them to their graves.

What starts there continues for policemen till they retire from their job. We are forced to see innumerable dead bodies, some out of demands of the law, some out of suspicion and some out of pure curiosity. The law mandates we inspect dead bodies and write a report on them. Some officers are mandated by rank to check on a few dead bodies, like those of married women dying unnaturally within seven years of marriage. Most accident cases are mandated to be checked and certified. So this journey of seeing dead bodies, and thereby people, has taken me to see some extraordinary human moments. Like the case of eighty-four-year-old woman jumping into her well and committing suicide only because her son settled in a faraway country and chose not to visit her for a long time. At that exact moment, I thought about my parents and how my job had taken me a state away. No amount of Facetime and WhatsApp video calls are a substitute for a personal visit to have quality time and a hearty meal with our near and dear ones.

I saw my first accident victim while I was a probationer—a college-going boy on a National Highway, driving a car and jumping the divider. We felt, based on the crime scene reconstruction, that he was possibly using his cell phone while driving. A momentary lapse of concentration, given the speed at which he was driving, made him enter the opposite lane and collide head-on with a lorry. There was nothing in the crime scene and all I could see was mangled metallic parts of the car and the young man's body strewn around. We had to collect all of the body parts in a gunny bag and take it to the hospital. The scene of his father, sitting inside the police station and writing the complaint, when the hospital staff were trying to stitch his son back into one piece to give back the semblance of a human being to him, broke me to my core. Despite my fervent pleas that procedures be completed later, the father wrote the complaint and gave it to the SHO. I was standing right behind him and he stood up, turned around and thanked me. For the first time, I broke down in my uniform in front of so many strangers.

There are also the heart-wrenching scenes of cases of school children committing suicide because of their teachers' pressure on them to succeed. In some cases, teachers are also booked under the law because of a suicide note and we could see the perplexed look on the teachers' faces, wondering what just hit them. In one moment, their life turned upside down and they went from a guru to a criminal.

Death, I have seen over the years, is the only true leveller. When death stares at you in the face, I guess other things that we chase start appearing meaningless. A family starting from their home on a long journey with all their loved ones, meets with an accident and right there, the world collapses for them. I have seen criminals getting killed by a rival gang hacking them to pieces because the dead had killed one of their criminal gang members the same way. The old and the wise cops around me would tell me, justice was served. At the same time, when some decent human beings get killed for no fault of theirs in accidents, the same cops have tried telling me that God has taken them to a better world. I didn't find any rhyme or reason for both of these events. I could only see men giving their lame justifications to satisfy themselves and our mind trying to fool us into believing that it had the answers for everything. The most important lesson for me, on witnessing death is this—life doesn't wait for anybody, it has its own mysteries.

So it is better to do what we have to do right now. Many of us have made our lives too complicated. Like Nelson Mandela in his book, *Long Walk to Freedom*, memorably said, 'As I walked out of the door (of my prison cell) to the gate that would lead to my freedom, I knew if I didn't leave my bitterness and hatred behind, I would still be in prison'. He said this after twenty-seven years of incarceration. Let us try and come out of our self-imposed jails and live our life fully. There is no guarantee that we have more days left in our account, as death is the only certainty in this infinite world of ours.

GAME CHANGERS

Understand—Dismantle—Rebuild

'You never let a serious crisis go to waste.'

- Rahm Emanuel

Our country urgently needs reforms at multiple levels. When reforms are undertaken in a piecemeal manner, it usually doesn't give the expected results. There is sclerosis that is set at the political level with little imagination to set a new direction and vision. The moment we go down to the level of the panchayat, we can see the quality of leadership in operation. Despite more than two decades of empowering local leaders, we still aren't able to create grassroots-level agents of change. With people's pressing needs dictating the political discourse rather than their aspirations, we seem to go from one crisis to another. The same can be said about our administrative structure as well. With the finances of our state being in a precarious condition, meaningful reforms are not possible without addressing governmental spending first. This is the era of welfare politics and politicians experimenting and fine-tuning the art of winning elections through their governmental spending. Bureaucrats have very little choice but to toe their political masters' lines. It's a crime when a state spends very little of their total budget on the creation of capital assets and more money on things that don't add any value. With the states' debt bill spiralling out of bounds, one shudders to think about our country and the path it is travelling now. Most of these ills can be attributed to the poor quality of leaders who lead us.

This chapter, titled 'Game Changers', is designed to take a serious look at some of the challenges we are confronting. Though it deviates from the topic of policing, all of these are important for two reasons. One, to truly understand where we stand with respect to our political, administrative and leadership abilities. And two, all of these have a direct bearing on policing and any reform that needs to be brought in. Addressing one without tackling the others is akin to keeping a patient on antibiotics without studying the root cause. I fervently believe that understanding the true dimensions of the problem will help us find solutions that are more practical, nuanced and implementable. More than anything else, 'Game Changers' is designed to help us understand the problem more than addressing it.

Police Reforms—Doing it with a Heart

Reforming our police force is being spoken about for a long time. In a multiparty democracy like ours, with federalism at its core, police reforms are a tough nut to crack. Police being a state subject with federal states having absolute and total control over it only adds to the complexity. The changes that are being envisioned have to cover all aspects connected to men in uniform. We need to reimagine the way police forces are being put to use to serve our public and the resources that are made available to them. The way police forces are being led by their own officers also needs to be scrutinised. Reforming them externally—by building them better buildings and providing them good vehicles—will not bring any change without the internal issues being addressed first. I believe a society that has set artificial standards for a specific set of human beings, like expecting a policeman to work sixteen hours a day and consciously regulating the working hours of a white-collar worker does justice to neither one of them. Policemen not complaining about their working conditions vociferously should not be construed as a reason for not doing enough for them.

With the lack of job opportunities elsewhere in the government, most of the constable recruitments attract postgraduates and sometimes even PhDs. These are the people, who after a basic training, which is also getting fast forwarded due to the extra ordinarily high number of vacancies across the states, enter the forces early and are expected to uphold the rule of law. Ninety-five per cent of this tribe's behaviour determines the common population's perception of the police. More often than not, the problems that come out and bring a bad repute also generate from this end. Unless reforms are brought in urgently, the state would be in trouble on both sides—the public to whom it is supposed to serve and the police, who are supposed to serve the state. We are seeing or have heard of umpteen issues of public getting abused at the hands of the police. This often happens in a public place like a traffic situation or during one's dreaded visit to police station. The language that is used, the carelessness with which one is treated, requiring a 'high level contact' even to get simple legal work done, have generated a high degree of aversion in the general public, which, in turn, makes the Indian police a less trusted body.

The men and women who wear the khaki uniform do it under extraordinary pressure and when we normally see them on roads, they invariably appear jaded, tired, unfit and most importantly, demotivated to work. In one study I did in the Chikkamagaluru district of Karnataka, when I was serving as its SP from August 2016 to October 2018, out of 1,151 personnel who had their mandated annual medical health check-ups conducted, close to forty-two per cent had hyper tension, forty-five per cent had diabetes, seventy per cent had fatty livers, twenty per cent had cardio related issues and three per cent had visual disorders. Almost ninety per cent were obese (BMI method).

According to an article published by the *The Times of India* in 2015, seventy-seven per cent of Bengaluru traffic cops suffer from vitamin-D deficiency.[1] I'm sure the data is similar everywhere. This is illuminating but equally shocking. Literally, most policemen are walking reminders of a profession that is burning them from the inside out, albeit slowly. The undue pressure on them, combined with long work hours without adequate breaks, is making this profession a more dangerous one than any peace-time job one could think of anywhere in the world. I'm certain that states which have larger vacancies like Uttar Pradesh and West Bengal might see more degrading effects of policing on their policemen's health.

In the beginning of my career, when complaints on my men reached me—simple ones like misbehaving with senior officers, being late for duty, being absent for duty, and some very serious ones like taking a graft from public for doing lawful work, assaulting a member of the public and violating human rights—my straightforward response was to be very harsh on them. I got a key insight in an incident which made me look deeper when I visited a policeman's house to check with his wife. There were frequent complaints of him beating his wife and also getting drunk but being present at work most of the time. During my inspection, I found

[1] Rajiv Kalkod. '77% Bengaluru traffic cops suffer vitamin D deficiency', *The Times of India*, 13 February 2015. https://timesofindia.indiatimes.com/city/bengaluru/77-Bengaluru-traffic-cops-suffer-vitamin-D-deficiency/articleshow/46221420.cms

all of the allegations to be true and I called him for an orderly room (a procedure where an errant policeman is called for enquiry and punishment is meted out). He turned out in his full uniform and fully drunk, as usual. He came in, saluted royally, apologised profusely and said he would not repeat his misconduct again. When I called for his file, I was truly shocked to see thirteen suspensions, increments postponed seven times in his salary and one rank reduction to his name. He was a fit case for dismissal. Something in me told me to go deep into his psyche. I offered him a chair to sit, he refused out of courtesy and I had to literally force him to sit. When I asked him, 'Tell me, how can I help you? You look miserable to me and you should help me to help yourself to come out of this misery.' He was shocked for an instant and started sobbing uncontrollably.

He poured out his whole life story—poverty in early life, surviving on a single meal per day, failing in his love life because of the duo belonging to different castes, joining the police, marrying a girl as per his parents' wish, the drift from parents for not being able to visit them regularly and finally, the realisation in the middle ages that his life was not going as per his plan. He also felt his son was going out of his hands. On top of it, to take his life back in control, he couldn't spend enough time with his family. In simple terms, he conveyed an important fact to me—that he had multiple faces to put up in life and he was struggling to hold on to even one correctly. The faces of being a father, a son, a husband and a police constable. Without doubt, because of his sixteen-hour workdays, he was forced to make this policeman facet override his other facets, failing in all of them and ultimately failing as a policeman as well. With nobody to listen and advise him, he got into the vicious cycle of depression which led to poor work performance and more suspensions and more depression.

Any work environment, if not designed properly, can wreak havoc with individuals and more than that, with their families. In this case, I had to put him in an alcohol de-addiction programme followed by a course in yoga. I made him get his rank back so that he could be at par with his batchmates who were promoted way ahead of him. I'm not saying that he turned out perfect, but he is improving and improving well. This was a unique case that helped me understand that people are complex entities by nature and treating any visible issue at the surface without an idea about the roots would be catastrophic. From then on, I started treating every case as a unique one, in many cases called officers to my home for a meal, if I found that something was off with them. During this honest conversation, invariably I was able to find that switch and the remedial measures to fix it and make it operational. If not attended right, we are barking up the wrong tree which will cause the organisation, and the individual, suffering till they are alive. An individual after leaving his day job, has to be home and perform his or her role as a parent. In some cases, as a son or daughter as well. There is a definite relationship between the personal and the professional and great corporates understand this and go all out to help their employees evolve into better human beings. Give them the deserved break, make them work a fixed weekly schedule, give them the enrichment needed to make their jobs meaningful. To put it more bluntly, I believe in the philosophy of treating our employees instead of customers, as Gods, so that they go out and do the same with our customers. Focusing too much on customers at the cost of our employees who give their blood and sweat, in my personal opinion, is a great disservice to our loyal soldiers who relentlessly keep marching.

In our political set-up with policemen being used as a tool for the men in power to extend their privileges, it's understandable that political will is not easily found to improve the conditions of the khaki and the policemen are treated as second-class citizens. I have also heard a politician on record saying that the government might focus on buying a bus for the transport department than a jeep for the police department as the former generates revenue unlike the later. This is also a painful reminder of the way a government functions with freebies, loan waivers, targeted spending going to the places or the population that votes for them and not to build capital assets that secures the future of any nation. With no capital asset creation for the state police barring a few jail buildings and police stations getting opened and some new vehicles replacing the worn-out old ones, the constabulary which comprises ninety-five per cent of the police force, still puts up with their heavy shoes, unfriendly headgear and wounded dignity. Less spending, combined with critical vacancy at the lower level (which increases their work load) creates a domino effect that washes away all the meaningful reforms taken at the local level by well-meaning officers.

While organisations around the world take pride in investing in their people—the most important asset—we invest very little in our most important resource. If we don't do that, how can we expect them to give their best every day? The policing budget, as a percentage of the state budget, is 3.56 per cent out of the total budget (2016–2017). Most of this allocation is to meet recurring revenue expenditures and very little is for capital expansion to give muscle to the police forces. Money that is put on training as a percentage of policing budget is around 1.03 per cent. This poor spending on training can be directly attributed to inefficiency in handling modern crimes, poor communication with stakeholders and a lack of expertise to do and deliver daily jobs well. What starts here only gets compounded further with the average vacancy of policemen across the lower ranks averaging out to twenty-seven per cent across the Indian states.

In a country where most institutions are not at their best, it's unfair to single out police as a failure and not giving it its rightful due. Also, with all of our attendant problems, it's actually a tough task to be a public servant as well. With most governments not managing their finances well, a public servant, especially a policeman, ends up at the bottom of the pay scale. Development needs take precedence over other needs and 'service' is emphasised in a public servant's life over 'salary'. With the other entrepreneurial sectors like the service sector on a continuous boom, public service at the higher levels, no more seems to be the first choice of employment for any young, aspiring graduate. This reduces the quality of replacement of the force that is retiring every year.

Public service, at this rate, might lose its critical edge of leading the nation with its vision and aspiration.

Also, with the state failing in the delivery of essential services to its citizens, a policeman, more often than not, is the rescuer and also the person who makes the state's writ visible. I have seen this countless times in my career, where policemen double up as electricity facilitators (when power goes off), municipal attenders (when municipality fails in some of their basic jobs), counsellors (though they are untrained) and life has taught them to solve all of the issues a common public faces—marital disputes, land boundary variations, religious fights, supporting the elderly and small settlements where the cost of taking it through a formal channel is not worth the trouble. In short, a policeman is our society's chief problem-solver. To put it simply, by making them do all of these jobs that are poorly defined and arise, in the first place, because of our other institutional failings, we are overburdening the policemen and expect too much out of them and may be beyond what they are capable off.

Despite all these issues of manpower and resource shortage, cultural strangleholds, lack of adequate periodic trainings and leadership deficiencies, I have seen many individuals who never allowed any of this to handicap them. The majority, if not all, continue to show empathy, decency, leadership and importantly the sense of duty in their daily working. Many a time they have amazed me by their efficiency by doing impossible jobs and repeatedly going beyond their call of duty. It more than anything had motivated me to be at my best or at least try to be at my best.

There is an incident that is close to my heart. The real power of determination, motivation and hard work was at play here. In one of our annual police sports meets, I asked a group of policemen, why our standards in sports were degrading. I could see a real lack of motivation and thereby lesser participation in the sporting events. One policeman replied, 'Sir, you can't expect me to come first by giving me one week's practice. I know that's not enough and the lack of interest starts there.' This made me think and I asked them what we could do to bring interest in fitness. The same person replied, 'Sir, give us some incentive. I'm sure it will work wonders.' After a few weeks of continuous mulling over, I felt I had a plan and wanted to test this interest at the weekly Friday parade. I announced the plan. It was slightly audacious and, I guess, had never been tried out anywhere—if our policemen reduced their weight, they could get transferred to a place of their choice. Initially, it was received with a sense of disbelief. Not only was it outside of the text books that were in operation till then, but my men weren't sure whether I would keep my word with all the pulls and pressures of the job.

About thirty-four personnel registered in year one with a three-month time to reduce 5 kgs or more. At the end of the ninetieth day, sixteen personnels were successful with an average reduction of 7 kgs. One person even reduced about 14 kgs. True to my word, I organised a small function to honour all those who had achieved their goal and all those who couldn't, but nevertheless tried. It was a revelation for me when some of them spoke. To reduce their weight, some of them altered their dietary habits and lifestyles. They started using their cycles or went on foot for shorter distances. They started taking packed lunches with them to eat on time. Out went the stress and in came yoga in their fitness routines. Our police line gym, with its bare minimum equipment, suddenly found takers in the morning. At the function, I honoured everybody with the transfers to their desired locations of their choice. When many questioned me or asked me, 'What, it is only weight reduction, right? What purpose is it going to serve?' My answer was always on the lines of, 'No. It's much more. We are fundamentally changing the belief system of a person. We are altering his thinking, his neural connections and this one-degree alteration is what all of us need to get our life back in order.' When the second year registrations opened, the registrations were in triple digits. That's the power of faith, belief and hard work, all combined. Can the change be real? Is it possible to build a culture of excellence with our khaki despite our shortcomings? I think it's possible, and we have an example for the perennial naysayers amongst us. Like the story that is about to follow.

I was in Bavaria, Germany in 2017 for a training programme with the German Police. The first thing I observed was the freshness of the German Police and how fit they were in addition to their typical German efficiency. They were alert, polite to a fault and most importantly, looked like the corporate types. These are things we do not associate with the Indian policemen, or any policemen, in fact. No wonder, the German police is amongst the most trusted non-political institutions in their country, much above universities and hospitals. It is a miracle that a police force originally created by

Adolf Hitler for a set-up that violated most aspects of humanity and which was sitting rock bottom in terms of public perception, has become a beacon for public institutions now. It has shown its ability to improve and adapt itself to a democratic set-up. In the last decade or so not only has it adapted but has also excelled among all the public institutions. Therein lies a little hope for our country as well. That change is possible and it only requires a strong conviction and the understanding that the time for change is now.

It all changed when a series of anti-police protests started against the police's heavy-handedness in handling unionised strikes in the late 1960s and a botched-up operation like the one to rescue a victim in a bank robbery. All of these culminated with the disastrous handling of the terrorist attacks during the Munich Olympics in 1972. This led to them being a global shame in front of a large TV audience and the country that takes pride in their identity felt let down massively. The government of the day constituted major police reforms immediately that included, attitudinal changes in the training methodology, removal of hierarchy in the forces, creation of a Special Forces unit for tasks that required a certain degree of finesse and building up world-class infrastructure for the German policemen and women. Though, Germany is a federal republic with an extraordinary amount of powers vested in its sixteen federal states, and policing being an important power given to those federal states, still a political will was found to undertake these major reforms during the early 1970s and another set of reforms post the 1989 unification. One could see the attitudinal changes that have happened over the years in the field and the way they behave with a common man. It's a common sight to see a member of the public buying a cop a mug of beer when he is off duty in the evening and the cop cooling his heels in a pub. Some of the recent reports even suggest that the German police also tops the aspirational workplace survey. I was also fascinated to see policemen of different ranks having a healthy respect for their senior officers but not genuflecting needlessly, having a healthy disagreement over issues and speaking truth to power when it mattered. The important take-away for me was their working hours—not more than eight hours per day. At whatever work they are engaged in, their replacement would be in and relieve them of their duties.

Because of their specialisation of the roles, one could see a remarkable progress in the reduction of crimes, pioneering work with the vulnerable youth population, border crimes, drug trafficking and domestic dispute resolution. Since the roles are well defined and the pay is quite good, they are the preferred place of employment for many college graduates. With fresh, educated talent that is equally driven, the German police have emerged as one among the best police organisations in the developed world.

Any meaningful police reform should start with restoring dignity to them, making them live normal lives first by giving them the opportunity to grow physically, intellectually, emotionally and spiritually. Anything that falls short is only like doing a disservice to these great people. The whole culture of denying the basic dignity to our lower-ranked police personnel in the name of discipline should be relooked at and a humane touch should be brought in. This will happen only when we force ourselves to do a fundamental rethinking of policing and the roles it entail. The Police Act of 1861 needs a thorough relook and two police-reform commissions and a Supreme Court mandated committee have spoken about this.[2] Though some of the reforms have taken place, these were only piecemeal. There is enough institutional knowledge inside the police department and with the correct set of leaders—who will allow their heart to override their mind, sometimes these changes can be brought in on a war footing. Their emotional needs as well as their family members' needs are to be attended. When leaves are granted on time, in a sense, the long working hours will not suffocate them. A culture of respect needs to be brought in. This culture that is generated will translate into huge gains—positive work atmosphere, clarity of thinking and executing critical jobs, lesser hospitalisations because of stress-induced illnesses and medical bills to be borne by the government, increased public respect and finally, a meaning to what they do on a daily basis.

It is also the state's duty to earmark time and resources to ensure that all policemen are physically fit. It cannot be left to the system or to a personal self-discipline regimen to be physically fit. With a sixteen-hour schedule, most of them might not have the time to follow a daily fitness regime. They live in

[2] Writ petition no. 310 of 1996, 417 of 2010, 42 of 2011 in Honourable Supreme Court of India. Case decided on April 11, 2011. http://dfs.nic.in/pdfs/PoliceReforms(E)181013.pdf

cramped accommodations and have no means to do simple acts like daily exercises in the places they live. Open-air gyms and walking tracks in police quarters have become necessary additions to their daily lives.

This has to be a combination of carrot and stick. Once the state starts spending resources on them, they are also expected to deliver. The physical markers, if not met, every five years or during promotion, the state should have the right to deny their promotion. For the IPS fraternity, the central government is trying to bring in a performance culture of fitness by classifying each of their fitness into SHAPE-1, SHAPE-2 and SHAPE-3. It should be the pride of a policeman to keep himself fit and efforts should be brought in on this front by him. Yes, this will entail a fixed initial expenditure for upgrading gyms at the district level and police quarters' level. But nothing comes cheap in life, right?

For their intellectual development, not much is happening as of now. They pass an exam during their recruitment cycle and many don't show an interest in keeping their knowledge up to date. Mainly, though, there is no proper Knowledge Management (KM) portal in place. Promotions from PC to HC and HC to an ASI and ASI to a SI and SI to an Inspector should be based on passing a certain qualifying exam. Till now, due to the exigencies of the job it has been considered okay to not have an intellectual rigour in the job. The time has come to redo the promotion and recruitment cycle. Also, psychological profiling to see the suitability for a role and a periodical refresher course—that compromises the latest in the policing field along with a course on ethics—should be brought in. This can be done with very little capital investment. Such initiatives are not taken because officials have become too busy with their daily work/chores.

The idea of having an eight-hour work day for the police is one that has been in discussion for a long time. To do this, the following things are needed—more recruitments (that is over the number of policemen who retire annually), improving the training capacity to train them and the immediate additional capital that is needed to pay salaries to all of these new recruits. With a five-seven-year vision plan and by getting the recruitment cycle right, an ambitious programme should be chalked out to bring their working time to an eight-hour schedule. With a political cycle that operates on a five-year plan, the last year of which goes in election management, a government ideally has got four years to make an impact. With most political leaders not willing to invest in a cause that will take more than two years minimum to show results, any visionary changes that propose a longer cycle to see fruits of labour get shunned. The key here, more than the finance to be mobilised, is to get this understanding passed on to the political executives, that this, if done well, will get them votes as this will be a definite game changer. At least for a start, the major cities can be quickly covered for this experiment and all we need is a commodity that is in short supply nowadays—political will.

Once, we are able to get this, a lot of attendant problems get solved automatically.

Reforms cannot be a one-way road and the time has come for the government servant to be more accountable than ever. Government jobs in India are only getting tested at the entry level and promotions are taken as a matter of right till retirement. Naturally, intellectual growth gets stunted as there is no incentive to improve. This has to change and police jobs have to be made competitive so that the best brains enter the service to solve our twenty-first century problems. Quality over quantity should be the mantra; jobs can be remapped and if needed, posts can be resized. Once this is brought in, the next step can be evolved to follow the British, Australian or any other suitable policing model, where everybody needn't be given a raise or promotion as a matter of right. The future of police organisation should thrive on a funnel approach, with only a certain proportion being promoted to their next ranks. Without having this, creating an intellectual culture where meritocracy plays a role will be tough. With India aiming to be a five trillion-dollar economy by 2025, we need to have a highly evolved, competitive and intellectually far superior police force to tackle those challenges that stand between now and the future growth.

The recent public support that the Indian policemen have rightly got because of their hard work and dedication in handling the COVID-19 situation, is a once-in-a-lifetime opportunity to change their image for good. Perhaps for the first time, people have embraced our khaki, shunning their fear and distrust. There is no better time than now, for administrators and political executives to give policemen what they had always asked for—a sense of dignity and meaning to their work.

Leadership—In Police and All around Us

I believe leadership is the single-most critical factor that influences any outcome. I believe in this maxim without a doubt and have seen this in countless instances. I have seen good leadership shown by the field officers—be it talking judiciously to two warring parties and calming them down or anticipating how things will shape up and getting the reinforcements ready or in way they maintain human relationships or dealing with any party with trust and integrity—preventing large scale riots and thereby, completely changing the expected outcomes. In many cases they were able to navigate themselves and their teams to a desired outcome. I also believe good leaders are rare—they are so rare, I can count some of the leaders with whom I had the privilege of working with in my policing career with my fingers. By leaders, I don't mean ranks, even though that's how the traditional leadership is defined, specially so, in uniformed services. I mean people sitting in any position of influence, big or small, and who are able to move the needle and make a difference. In this world that is becoming complex, ambiguous, volatile and uncertain, good leadership, without any doubt, assumes critical importance. I fundamentally believe leadership, as a philosophy, when applied correctly, can make our relationships joyful, our lives purposeful and the world a more meaningful place.

For a long time, leadership revolved around military context and its generals. The available literature on leadership focused on getting things done, leading our people and keeping a group well-knit and run tightly. At its core, leadership is all about caring for others, helping the people around us to be better and in the process, we bettering ourselves. Everyone requires leadership, whether in a large or small capacity. In the last couple of decades, the meaning of leadership has become twisted and somehow it has been associated with the image of an aggressor with cowboy machismo. It has also become more bottom-line oriented, focusing exclusively on outcomes, titles and designations, not driven by emotions and certainly not by the intangibles like courage, faithfulness and team spirit. The world has become a poorer place because of this distortion and the younger generation is still getting schooled in the post-Second World War assembly line production concept of 'getting things done fast'. I believe the time is right to bring in care, empathy, compassion and authenticity to the table and weave it into our action-oriented leadership world.

In the initial years of my service, I was curious and would lap up books written by American military generals about leadership—its key ingredients, how people behaved across eras, how a single personality was able to change the course of history. This was mostly because those were the only books I could find and were invariably written by American historians. The great George Washington, who commanded the continental army in the American Revolutionary War, taught me that leadership is all about tactical brilliance and never losing sight of the larger vision in the fog of war; the peerless Robert E Lee was all about moral choices, sacrifices and a high sense of duty; the redoubtable Douglas MacArthur was all about strategy and managing the complex moving pieces. But it was with General Pete Pace, General David Petraeus and General Stanley McChrystal that I associated more as I was able to relate to them and their work in the last two decades. It was a surreal moment for me when I read that General Pete Pace, who retired as the Chairman of the Joint Chiefs, on his last day on the job, headed to the Vietnam War Memorial and left his four stars to his fallen comrades with this note:

General Pete Pace's letter to his fallen comrades

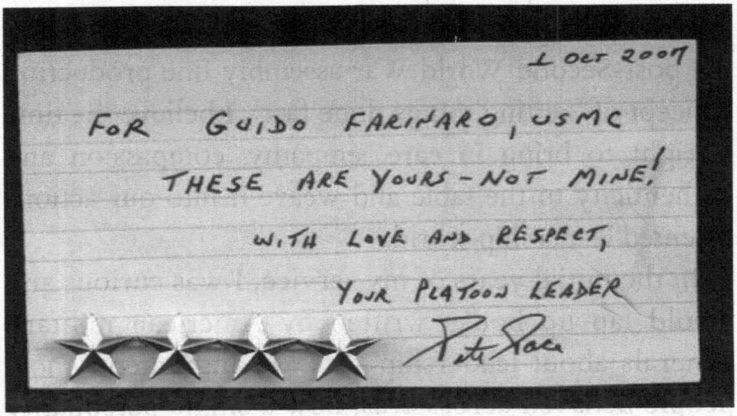

A General, on the last day of his career, was thinking about his comrades on whose shoulder he was able to climb and go all the way up. This incident, for me, was an extraordinary demonstration of loyalty, authenticity, selflessness and the true spirit of being a soldier. General David Petraeus was all about out-of-the-box thinking and was a master at fighting insurgencies. His book, *All In—The Education of General David Petraeus*, is a fascinating read on the complex times after 9/11 and the inspiring leadership that he demonstrated in Iraq and Afghanistan. But it was perhaps from General Stanley McChrystal that I derived a lot of daily inspiration. He was a soldiers' general who broke the back of the Al-Qaeda in Iraq in his initial years and took on the Taliban insurgency later in Afghanistan. It was by piecing together his service and life that I was able to deeply appreciate team loyalty, empowerment and creating teams, just like his book, *Team of Teams*. I learned from this general that leadership, when sowed with empathy, empowerment and goal-oriented action, will produce remarkable results in all facets of our life.

I was able to bring in my sense of leadership in the field and was lucky enough to put that into action. For starters, there is no hiding for leaders in Indian police set-up. We are surrounded by people and policemen all the time. Our personal actions are scrutinised and labeled. The excesses committed by our family members in the name of our powers are accepted grudgingly. if there is no praxis in our own actions and thoughts, we can't expect those around us to practice what we preach. In policing, personal leads the professional meaning personal habits go a long way in shaping up our professional acceptance. Luckily, I had an understanding family that was able to see this and gave their fullest support. The men under my command were empowered to the level my office allowed me to. A transparent office set-up was put in place to exhibit fairness, integrity and probity when we were dealing with officers' grading and their performance. I might have strayed the path occasionally but never with any mala fide intention.

For a police man, leading means demonstrating the virtues or principles that are expected of everyone who wear a uniform. Collaborating might entail the leader to work cutting across departments and breaking internal silos. Rallying will be to bring all of the ranks to a common vision and direction. All of these can be done in a straight jacketed way through rules or procedures or with empathy and understanding. The underlying ingredient is whether you do this act by your head or by your heart or by a combination of both. When I relook leadership in my police career, I always felt leadership at its root is being caring and being authentic. We might not know that we are straying but a smart observer can easily smell out the nature of a leader like the sweat in our arm pits. Leadership like in any field, also comes in policing in two dimensions—Bad and Good.

A few years back, a senior police officer visited a district where I was serving. As the tradition demands, an escort car was sent to receive him and escort him to the headquarters. On arrival, his first words were, 'Anna, your men have become *dheela* (loose) like you'. Hiding my discomfort, I asked him, 'Why sir?' His prompt reply was, 'I found your men are not saluting me properly. Their hands are not in the exact ninety-degree position.' He further gave his own remedy as well, 'I remember when I was an SP like you, I made one police constable to do mock salutes a thousand times in my office. So that others got a lesson.' I mumbled my answer and tried diverting the topic. In another case, a very senior officer suspended a (Station House Officer) SHO for as petty an issue as he not being taken care of well by that SHO. The senior officer took his ire out on the poor SHO when he demanded liquor it was not made available to him in the middle of the night—that too when prohibition orders were in force. There are many police leaders who are more takers than givers. Takers in the sense of taking more out of their job and titles and giving less in terms of leadership.

In numerous cases, a policeman is made to wait for an infinite number of hours to meet a senior officer because the hierarchy system in the senior's office demands that he wait and earn his time as he is too junior to immediately walk in. When we go down the hierarchy, the same issue manifests in different forms across ranks like an SHO demanding that you stand in front of him, a traffic cop getting restless the moment you start arguing with him or in an extreme case, the public getting assaulted for not giving the 'required respect' to a man in uniform. If one carefully analyses the root causes of these behaviors, we can understand that authority is not in tandem with honour, transparency and empathy. Leadership is also operating in terms of power, machoism and inauthenticity. This over a point of time creates a culture that is static and once it sets in, starts encouraging people to behave in way of the 'in-group' and existing culture. Even the young recruits who enter the force quickly adapt themselves so that they are not shunted to the 'out-group' and made a pariah.

Bad leadership also manifests when proactive measures are not in place to prevent unwanted things from occurring or not quickly mitigating them when they happen. I remember learning a lesson on this very early in my career. When I was the SP of a district in coastal Karnataka, I used to take a one-and-a-half-hour lunch break out of a twelve-hour schedule. When I returned to office one day, I saw one old head constable with tears in his eyes waiting in the visitor's room. When I asked what the problem was, he replied that his father had passed away. Taken aback, I asked him what was he doing there and why he wasn't at his home. His reply literally tore me apart. He said, 'Sir, I belong to northern part of Karnataka and I work here. I asked for a twenty-day leave from my SHO but he was willing to give me only ten days. I can't come back again to extend it. So, I thought of asking you to give me the leave at one shot.' A person, on the worst day of his life, after losing someone very close, believed in the so-called hierarchy and was waiting for me. I kicked myself for allowing this to happen to him. This was purely an avoidable incident, if only the mitigating measures had been put in place. The first thing I did post this incident was to put in place a revised leave policy and empowered the individuals to self-sanction it, provided it met the pre-informed conditions. This also put me on a course to do a lot of soul-searching and to delegate as much as possible and hold my officers and men accountable when needed. Not being proactive or not considering mitigating an issue by anticipating it, was to me, an example of bad leadership.

Bad leadership is generally observed only after the occurrence of an event. Humans by nature have too many blind spots and don't realise when bad leadership is in operation, like allowing a woman to travel at night all alone from an IT company in Bengaluru at 2 AM. Till the moment an incident of a rape or murder happens, nobody seems to care about the safety of women. Things will get corrected in toto when we all jump in together, including the government, after the occurrence of an incident. This is only because we are not trained to think about putting measures in place to mitigate risks even before the occurrence of an incident by anticipating it. Adding to this, we have stopped thinking consciously about the people for whom we are responsible.

With increasing financial misdeeds in corporate settings, one can also parallelly see that the performance appraisal is increasingly being driven by achieving financial targets. This generally builds in a culture of encouraging shortcuts to achieving results, or in the worst case, the companies themselves looking the other way provided the targets are met. One fine day, the whole edifice will collapse. No wonder, financial frauds are at an all-time high now. Most of the cases of theft in workplaces or servant thefts happen again because of bad leadership. We don't have adequate systems in place to catch somebody when they steal a nominal amount. We only shout from the rooftops when we see everything around us is gone.

Bad leadership can be avoided only if we treat every single outcome—good or bad—as an opportunity learn; to keep fine-tuning systems anticipating problems, to put in place proper mitigation measures for when there's a lack of anticipation and so on. Bad leadership happens because of our lack of consciousness, not treating our roles with the care and attention they deserve and not willing ourselves to make that extra difference to whatever we do. I personally believe analysing and studying bad leaders has taught me more about leadership. Failures and critical analysis of an event or outcome teach us valuable lessons.

I have seen many disturbing cases of policemen not being cared for and in worst cases, even insulted. This sense of worthlessness leads to many of the larger problems we see among the uniformed men. For example, in the present context, we see policemen threaten to go on mass leave, organise protests in front of their superiors' offices, and in some unimaginable cases, gun down their seniors. With the penetration of social media, all policeman irrespective of their rank, believe their voice needs to be heard. They also expect that they be led well and taken care of.

All of these instances are a daily reminder of the quality of leadership that is at play and the importance we give to creating and nurturing the fast diminishing breed of 'good leaders'.

Good leadership is tough to define as one can control everything and still, the results might not come along as expected. So the outcomes might not necessarily define a good leadership. Good leadership can mean the presence of a boss whose company we enjoy and don't dread. Work doesn't appear to be a chore anymore and we enjoy doing it because we are able to connect it to a larger purpose. It's also the feeling that you are willing to slog that extra as you don't want to let down the people who trust you. Good leadership is all about caring and being authentic with people around us. I still remember the example a senior police officer gave me on caring. Consider a situation where you sanction leave to one of your men on the grounds of his family member being unwell. On his return to work, if you ask him about the condition of his relative's health, it would be a simple gesture of showing you care for that person. This is the bare minimum to start with for an officer whose main job is to take care of people around him.

People flocked to Gandhi because he genuinely cared for those around him. Though it took thirty-two years after him landing in India in 1915, to get independence, Gandhi was able to build a powerful narrative about the larger cause only by his authenticity. Slowly but steadily, he was able to attract large numbers of people from all walks of life to his camp. In this world where everything is about 'me', we genuinely refuse to see the other person's point of view and that's why we see marriages collapsing, societal strife increasing, office politics rising, and last but not the least, we have also lost the sense of inner balance.

Good leadership starts with 'us' and not 'me'. The reason KPS Gill was able to rally his men around him during the worst phase of Punjab militancy was that he cared for his men. In turn, his men took on his mission as theirs and brought an end to a seemingly insurmountable problem. One of the main reasons the elusive forest brigand, Veerapan, was hunted down by the Tamil Nadu Special Task Force in 2004 was only due to the superior leadership that was provided to them. K Vijay Kumar, who was its chief then, was able to make his men rally around his mission. In his book, *Veerapan: Chasing the Brigand*, one could clearly picture him in action and how he was one among his men in terms of doing their routine duties. Despite being the chief, he insisted on doing the sentry duty at camps, slept with his men in the jungles, removed the concept of ranks while leading teams inside and purely went by the guy who he thought could get the job done. No wonder, when the time came, his boys were willing to be part of the final dangerous operation to penetrate into Veerapan's inner circle.

The greatest of police leaders who led me had authenticity at their core. They were transparent. They never gave orders with ulterior motives. Teams trusted them and were absolutely willing to get the job done without worrying about any inevitable repercussions. Most conversations with them would inevitably start around personal aspects and would then enter the professional realm.

Another question that I had frequently confronted during my policing career was about balancing one's emotions with rationality. A force that is built on its unique ability to self-discipline itself cannot compromise its discipline at any cost as the whole edifice will crumble if the basic component is taken out. I remember going after people in my office headquarters if they turned up late (we were using an automated attendance system). When I usually called for an explanation before any action was initiated, the following are the common reasons I got:

1. Taking care of old parents, cooking their lunches and other such issues. This is apart from supporting their spouses and getting their children ready for school.
2. Travelling for over an hour in a government bus (in early morning peak hour traffic) one way.

Though some of the reasons can be classified as 'silly' because of the personal nature of the work, it's also important to understand that the personal is professional most of the time. If our colleagues were to be sitting inside their workspace with personal issues occupying their mind space, they would not be in a position to give their best at work. This is something I was able to appreciate over time and devised some practical ways to handle it. Flexibility in their working hours was brought in for new mothers and those with other parental duties. An extended afternoon break was considered in other cases. All of these, it felt, didn't require great thinking but only the right intentions. Seeing anybody as a true human being is seeing them as a combination of their job titles, personal titles and social titles. When approached from that angle, miracles do occur as we are seeing situations from a completely changed perspective. This approach is much-needed to humble ourselves and to remember that fates could reverse and people at the top could always find themselves at the bottom of the rung.

We all know the story of MK Gandhi being thrown out of a train in Pietermaritzburg in South Africa. There is an important lesson that is hidden right inside it and which we might miss if we don't get the context right. The incident that happened on 7 June 1893 is worth looking at again. Gandhi was thrown out of a train despite having a valid ticket for travelling in a first class compartment. Gandhi recalls this incident, 'It was winter and winter in the higher regions of South Africa is severely cold. Maritzburg being at a high altitude, the cold was extremely bitter. My overcoat was in my luggage, but I did not dare ask for it lest I should be insulted again, so I chose to shiver. I began to think of my duty. The hardship to which I was subjected was superficial, only a symptom of the deep disease of colour prejudice.'[1] That one night spent in the cold railway station possibly transformed this young lawyer into a 'Mahatma'. Not only did he take on the South African government, but he also shook the foundations of the British Empire in India, fought for our country's independence and achieved it. Later, a whole host of leaders followed Gandhi's path to free their countries from colonial oppression.

This transformation of MK Gandhi to Mahatma Gandhi happened when he was able to surmount his 'me' to a large cause. Very rarely can human beings do that and Gandhi was an exception along with a few others. In our daily lives, we all can try to rise above our narrow selves and identify ourselves with our purpose. This can be equally relevant when trying to be a good manager, a good CEO, a good police officer or a good politician. I fundamentally believe that this is the path that has to be taken if we truly want to become

[1] MK Gandhi. *An Autobiography: The Story of My Experiments with Truth by M K Gandhi*, 'Chapter 32: On my Way to Pretoria', Dover Publications, 1983.

good leaders, free ourselves of our petty egos, and truly dedicate our lives to change the direction of this world when we are in a position to do so.

To summarize, most men in uniform live on a certain credo. The credo where 'our men' takes precedence over its leaders under any circumstances. This is only possible when this credo is drilled into any leader who aspires to lead us. On the walls of the National Defence Academy (NDA), Dehradun, and attributed to Field Marshal Philip Chetwode, 1st Baron Chetwode, who formally inaugurated the Indian Military Academy in 1932, while he was Commander-in-Chief India, one will find this quote:

'The safety, honour and welfare of your country come first, always and every time. The honour, welfare and comfort of the men you command come next. Your own ease, comfort and safety come last, always and every time.'

No words can better capture the essence of good leadership.

Politics—Reformation Starts with Better Understanding

Politics and politicians are intertwined with the daily lives of all classes of Indians. The economically and socially well-off are the participants in the electoral arena, they are part of political parties and occupy important positions in the party apparatus. Some of them have even started their own political parties to secure their interests as well to strengthen their hold in the community. Many of our leaders have a mass following and for many others it's a mantle that is passed down from generation to generation. When power gets transferred on a mantle, the charismatic ones among them make it big and the less able ones at least maintain a base to keep their dynasties afloat. The other classes of people, mostly the lowest strata, are the foot soldiers. These loyalists are the fulcrum on which political parties operate. They do all the hard work and keep the ideology of the party running through their bloodlines. More than anything, they are invariably present in all party meetings in their area and give their leaders the muscle power when needed. Come election time, they are much in demand as not only do they make up the numbers but also do the much-needed heavy-pulling for canvassing.

The middle ones belong to the huge middle-class population. They passively participate in all the Indian elections, faithfully vote for a candidate of their choice and are the vast majority around whom the political communication revolves. Politics is very closely followed in India and nobody is out of its clutches. Indian democracy also seems to throw an astonishing number of leaders into the political arena. Some are able to stand the heat and dust of Indian politics while others fade away as quickly as they come. Before talking about political reforms, it's important to understand how politicians are formed in this heat and dust and what work they do.

This is a story of two fascinating Indian politicians. The first one, Dean Kuriakose is a politician from Idukki and is its current Member of Parliament (MP). Among the sitting MPs, he has got the highest number of cases against his name. As per his affidavit, he has a total of 204 criminal cases against him. Some of the crimes range from culpable homicide not amounting to murder, house trespass, robbery, criminal intimidation etc. He also won this election with a margin of 171,053 votes for the Indian National Congress (INC) party. He is just thirty-eight years old and is expected to have a long political career. The other politician is from the eastern parts of Uttar Pradesh, known as the badlands of Indian politics. A one-time MP and five-time Member of Legislative Assembly (MLA) from Mau (and also a sitting MLA now), his name is Mukhtar Ansari. He had spent the better part of the last decade in UP jails for murdering the sitting MLA of Ghazipur in 2005. Also, two of his elections were won from inside the jail with very little campaigning outside. Not only in Mau, he holds considerable clout among the Muslim community in the eastern part of Uttar Pradesh as well. He holds sway over close to twenty seats in that area through his own party, Qaumi Ekta Dal (QED). Now, we will analyse both of these leaders—one from the northern and the other from the southern part of India to see what ails Indian politics and some measures to reform it.

I'm sure with the data that is presented, most of us have painted a picture of both of these politicians and Indian politics in general. But when I present to you the next set of data, your perspective of them might change.

Dean Kuriakose is the former president of INC's Youth Congress-Kerala unit and a lawyer by profession. This is his first term as MP as well. The Indian politicians in general seem to have high number of cases against them and he is not an exception to this. One of the main reasons is that our politics is generally confrontational by nature. This is a form of political tool that has been in use right from the early part of the 1900s. In the confrontational style of politics, opposing ideologies confront each other to garner public attention. Sometimes this ends up in a street fight and at other times, in a large law and order issue. Cases are generally filed by the police for breaching public peace, rioting, unlawful assembly etc. If we look at Dean Kuriakose's parliament achievements very closely, he is without any doubt an above-average performer. His attendance is close to ninety-five per cent vs the national average of eighty-five per cent; he has participated in twenty-six debates vs the national average of sixteen and a half; and, he has asked sixty-two questions vs the national average of forty-nine. There is one more interesting statistic that is hidden inside his election affidavit. Out of the 204 cases against him, 193 cases are registered for a single incident. All of these were registered against him for the hartal called by INC party for the murder of two youth congress workers in Kasargod, Kerala on 18 February 2019. He was made a co-accused in all the places where the hartal was called and the police registered a suo moto case, as the hartal was against the court order. As a matter of fact, when I studied all of his 204 cases ranging from 2016 to 2019, I found that almost all of these were connected to the politics at ground. Though some of the sections were serious ones, like house trespassing and Kerala's local act that penalises damage to a private property, it was not done with any personal animosity to another person. The Indian media conveniently set a narrative based on the cases that were registered and thereby painted most of the politicians as criminals. This not only does injustice to the politics that is currently in operation in India but also to our understanding of it.

The table below contains data showing the number of cases that the sitting MPs of the past three Lok Sabha elections have had against them[2]:

Year	*Criminal cases against members*	*Serious criminal cases against members*
2009	162	76
2014	185	112
2019	233	159

[2] Public data available based on the affidavit submission at the time of filing nomination.

Again, this data might not give an accurate picture and when I checked on some of these serious criminal cases, specifically for grave offences and offences against women, the following is the data, I could muster: in the current Lok Sabha, out of the 543 members, eleven have cases of murder against them, thirty have cases of attempt to murder, nineteen members have cases of offences against women including three members for rape and six for kidnapping. Also, twenty-nine members have cases against them for hate speech. These are the members I would be worried about the most.

This in a way gives a clear picture of Indian politics, the way that it is in operation now. In our democracy, where the institutions are performing sub-optimally, including the government agencies, many people turn to capable politicians who can get the job done. Some of the capable politicians are street fighters willing to take up cudgels some time for a people's cause and many a time to keep themselves relevant.

As Milan Vaishnav argues in his brilliantly written book, *When Crime Pays,* on the interplay between criminals and Indian politics, 'On the other hand, voters consciously elect such candidates for their ability to "get things done". In the face of a weak rule of law and salient social divisions, the criminality of candidates gains credibility among voters, who rely on criminal politicians to protect their interests and to act like the crutch that helps them "navigate a system that gives them so little access in the first place". Over a point of time, this seems to be an advantage for all of these politicians as their ability to get the job done and also stand in the street for a common man becomes an insurmountable advantage for them. Candidates linked with criminal activities have strong chances of winning-a candidate with the criminal case is, on an average almost three times more likely to win elections against the candidate who faces no case.' From our analysis, we can infer that criminal cases being filed against you comes with the territory of being a politician and trying to navigate the institutional failures.

The second politician falls in the other end of the spectrum. Mukhtar Ansari, the current MLA of Mau, UP is not our ordinary politician. He has got close to forty cases registered against him, ranging from murder and kidnapping to rioting. The most brazen and the daring one is the day light shooting and murder of the then sitting MLA of Ghazipur, Krishnanand Rai and six of his supporters. After a lot of hue and cry, this case was finally taken over by the CBI and Mukhtar Ansari was formally arrested in 2009. He made Mau a pocket borough of his family and he was able win five times, twice as an independent. He later started his own party, QED, and has been in an alliance with Mayawathi's Bahujan Samajwadi Party (BSP) 2017 onwards. His brother, Afzal Ansari, is also a sitting MP from Ghazipur. Mukthar Ansari has been in jail for almost a decade and managed to win elections without campaigning. How is it possible? Do people wantonly vote for a known 'criminal'? Here, we have to be a little careful again before we make assumptions. As was quoted in an article, 'So, what explains the political clout of the Ansari brothers? The answer lies in their "connect" with the poor people through gram pradhans in these areas. "If you need their support to get medical treatment or settle marriage of your daughter or performing other rituals, you can just communicate to the pradhan. His men will be at your doorstep to extend all help…".[3]

With both the brothers emerging as the faces of Muslim community of eastern UP and the Mau assembly constituency itself comprising of twenty-four per cent Muslim population, they are, in general, seen by the people as go-getters.

The other interesting point that we gather from the Ansaris and many other similar stories is this—generally the voting public are not swayed by TV-channel debates and elitist versions of right and wrong. They need somebody who can get the job done and can pull in authority to make the government officers work. All of these politicians have to have their skin in the game or else people would just vote them out and push them away. In a strange twist, the main accused in the murder of the MLA in 2005, Munna Bajrangi, and a close associate of Mukhtar Ansari, was murdered inside a jail in 2018. On July 2019, the special CBI court had acquitted Mukhtar Ansari and his brother on all charges of murder for lack of evidence. What gets stranger is this: Mukhtar Ansari's grandfather was the former president of INC and Muslim League during the Indian Independence Movement and the former vice-president of India, Hamid Ansari, is his cousin.

[3] Sanjay Singh. 'Poll pourri: Local dons carve out their dens in eastern UP', *The Economic Times*, 27 February 2017. https://economictimes.indiatimes.com/news/politics-and-nation/poll-pourri-local-dons-carve-out-their-dens-in-eastern-up/articleshow/57363556.cms?utm_source=contentofinterest&utm_medium=text&utm_campaign=cppst

These two personalities are easily among the common representations of an Indian politician. With corruption in our democracy acting as a strong entry barrier, most democracies have lost their sense of newness with only a few people lording over it. Unfortunately, corruption in democracy is as old as democracy itself. The philosopher Epictetus (I CE) made this telling comment on the state of electoral politics in ancient Rome:

> 'For the sake of these mighty and dignified offices and honours you kiss the hands of another man's slaves—and are thus the slaves of men who are not free themselves. . . . If you wish to be consul you must give up your sleep, run around, kiss men's hands, rot away at other men's doors. . . send presents to many and daily xenia [guest-gifts] to some. And what is the result, twelve bundle of rods, sitting three or four times on the tribunal, giving games in the circus, and distributing meals in little baskets.'[4]

The current Indian politicians seem to be no better. Though we can list out many reasons for corruption in politics, one of the main reasons seem to be the humongous cost involved in contesting elections. Naturally, this attracts a certain set of candidates, who have the money bags with them to take care of themselves and the party as well. The political leaders have an unenviable task to balance between the so-called good and bad candidates. The criminal politicians are

[4] Fergus Miller. 'Epictetus and the Imperial Court', *The Journal of Roman Studies*. 55: (1/2). 141–148. https://www.jstor.org/stable/297436

able to mobilise the money and in many cases, they are in politics to protect their ill-gotten wealth. As a side-effect, this leads to an increase in criminality in politics. Again quoting from Milan Vaishnav's wonderfully researched book, '...the demand for criminal politicians by political parties can be understood on the basis of the soaring costs of election campaigns, which parties are unable to afford. Therefore, parties increasingly look for candidates who not only self-finance their campaigns, but also add to the party coffers and line the pockets of party elites. What do the criminals get in return, "by directly contesting elections, criminals could reduce the uncertainty associated with negotiating (and renegotiating) contracts." Criminals thus join politics for self-preservation, protection, and the potential financial benefits they stand to gain by holding office.'

With many political parties becoming masters of election management and election costs skyrocketing, most candidates cannot but fail to meet the election expenditure ceiling fixed by the Election Commission of India (ECI). The mandated ceiling limit for an Assembly election at this point of time is ₹28 lakhs and for the Lok Sabha elections is ₹70 lakhs. With ECI pouring more observers to monitor the election processes right down to the micro level, politicians find ingenious ways to spend that money and in some cases even bribe the voters, without getting caught. The politicians seeming to be one step ahead of the monitoring officers and the election process in India continues to be a cat and mouse game with the administration only playing catch up. Only a handful of elected politicians across the Indian electoral landscape have been disqualified for exceeding their spending limit; the common man cannot just dream of winning an Indian election, even if his head and heart are in the right place. In the just-concluded Lok Sabha elections, the number of winners with a declared income of crore and above were 443 out of 543 (at eighty-two per cent) whereas ten years or two terms previously, in 2009, it was 315 out of 443 (at fifty-eight per cent). They are the crorepati candidates and members of our venerable institutions.

The main reason for corruption creeping into politics is human greed. This is found across all human endeavours, where men who are in a positions of power and with very little oversight by the systems, make it a habit to enrich themselves. Political offices are no better, with ambiguity built in the decision making process and added to it the huge power their office holds, many of them indulge in reckless acts of corruption. Some of them, after getting caught, go through the long-winded Indian criminal justice system and many seem to escape the law.

In a country like India, the politicians most often seem to do a job, for which they are not elected. They are elected to be law makers but they mostly only solve petty issues (and sometimes serious issues). The people have also made politicians accountable as they need to have their 'skin in the game' and are expected to jump in and solve problems. Officers, by the very nature of their job, are not always accountable to the public and with some northern states having serious governance issues, naturally a strong politician or a 'Bahubali' rises. People also seem to have a liking for criminals and other strongwilled individuals as they tend to force their way through and get the job done either legally or illegally. That's why we see that those states which have better governance mechanisms, hardly see the rise of 'Bahubali' politicians. The quality of politicians in India is to a larger extent dependent on the quality of the governance mechanism that is present at the local level. The moral wish of having 'good and neat' politicians on the ground might not be appealing to the people as their needs are much different than that of the educated elites. Till the governance mechanism improves, which at best is sketchy, in many of our states, we cannot prevent the rise of strongwilled individuals with a criminal background occupying important political positions. Whatever laws are made to stop their rise, the same system will help them emerge from the crevice in the gaps in governance. Also, with dynasties dominating Indian politics, the real meaning of democracy is being lost in many constituencies. The other concern is the rise in the number of electoral constituencies becoming family pocket boroughs, and being run like mini republics. But the local population doesn't seem to be mindful of that. The locals also seem to relish it as they tend to get a dependable person free of petty corruption and things get done as the officers also know that these politicians are there to stay.

Immediately after our independence, in the first national elections, most of the candidates were reluctant politicians. People just voted for the INC party without even caring who stood where. In the first ever general election to the Lok Sabha in 1951, there were only 17.3 crore registered voters and the voter turnout was 45.7

per cent. Over the subsequent elections, with single party democracy giving way to a multiparty democracy, many castes started producing assertive leaders. As Rajni Kothari argues in his defining book, *Caste in Indian Politics*, the role caste groups play in Indian politics has exponentially increased post the collapse of Congress party as a system. Castes have been deep-rooted in India for a long time, dating back many centuries and we can ignore this only at our own peril. With the Mandal commission report and the politics around it generating the next wave, and the current wave mostly characterised by the affluent, Indian politics undergoes seismic changes every decade.

To complete what we started, Mukthar Ansari, whom we have analysed in detail, made an attempt to contest Lok Sabha elections in 2014 from Varanasi against the BJP prime ministerial candidate, Narendra Modi. The INC party decided to nominate a five-time MLA and a local strong man, Ajay Rai. In a strange coincidence, at the last moment, Mukthar Ansari decided to withdraw from the contest to help Ajay Rai, thereby preventing the division of votes. At that point of time, Mukthar Ansari was cooling his heels in jail for the murder of the sitting BJP MLA from Ghazipur, Krishnanand Rai, in 2005. Ajay Rai, the INC candidate, happened to be the brother of the deceased MLA. Can there be stranger bed fellows than these?

Enough is said about the ills of Indian democracy and the politicians who populate it. At the same time, this democracy has also truly delivered when it was fortunate to get some good leaders. We have significantly lifted millions out of poverty and improved standards of living for a vast majority of our population. But if one were to survey the Indian political landscape now and assess where we truly stand, the signs would not be very encouraging. Caste groups and their leaders dominate the way votes are polled and decide who gets to win a seat. Once they get elected, more energy goes into managing their folks and to prevent any leader from emerging and becoming their competitor. Demagoguery has taken over our democracy with empty promises and catchy slogans with very little accountability. Essentially this means a democracy keeps electing its leaders based on their familiarity and not necessarily on their vision. To change this we cannot blame the public who elect their leaders but the aspiring politician who is offering himself before the voter.

Again it takes us back to the simple question. What does a voter need? They need somebody who is approachable, has the ability to solve their problems, is empathetic to their situation, and most importantly, trustworthy. All these are qualities that are in short supply in our wider world even though we need them in large numbers. Since the aspiring leaders are not able to show cause or don't have this, the average Indian voter simply shuns them away. They become one election wonders—having the right intentions but not having the stamina to stay in the electoral arena for some more time. Twenty-first century India has plenty of problems. Its starts with our basic issues—food, housing and mobility. These needs are to be tackled with a very vigorous reimagination of solutions to the same problems. Even after seventy odd years post our Independence, we still have people who can't take their food for granted and have to worry about their next meal. Leaders have to find efficient ways to improve their social security net, find a way to target these groups effectively and make sure they don't slip back into the same place from where they climbed up. These require laws which will not speak the language of bureaucracy but empathy and a thorough understanding of the ground. If we look at the other problems in front of us, our cities have become unliveable with mobility becoming a big mess. Thanks to our unorganised planning and short-term approach for a long time. Now is the time to detangle this problem and to make our cities sustainable, breathable and liveable. To do this, we need leaders who are confident of themselves and willing to take the necessary risks, even if it might appear electorally unsound. These problems need thorough fixing and new solutions. Sometimes, these solutions could be leap-frogging or incremental. But finally, it boils down to the political will as implementation of bold steps will create a short-term jerk or pain. Even when the citizens are unwilling to go through the grind, responsible leaders can lead and show a way.

The other pressing issue we have is the increasing division among ourselves. Though we are united by a country and a common spirit of being an Indian, a significant population still chooses its other identities over this. Technology, that is supposed to bring us together, is creating the rift and making our people more polarised. Social media applications that are supposed to shrink this world have weaponised our words and thoughts. These are the gaps the leaders prey on and use it to their advantage. The worrying trend is the widening of these gaps. We need leaders who are healers, broad minded and in possession of a sense of responsibility to the offices to which they are elected.

Now, time and again many young guys ask me about the state of Indian politics and express their interest in cleaning this up. The only thing I tell them is to go to the grassroots and take one issue at a time and try to address it completely. Not only do I suggest solving the issue but also to make sure that the solutions for it are sustainable. The grassroots in India have got problems in millions and are waiting for people with the right intentions to set all the ills plaguing us - right.

There are serious issues with our agricultural set-up. Forces that are operating from global to local arena have made agriculture unsustainable and less lucrative for a vast majority of our Indian farmers. I'm seeing this at the grassroots level because of the work our foundation is doing. Solving most of these require changes in our law and goes right up to our understanding of a farmers' problem. Many a times, we seem to throw up solutions to problems that we don't even understand correctly. Likewise, in education and the way our students are trained, I see a need for the complete remodelling of our education set-up. While our education system is designed to focus on teaching and learning, the job market is expecting them to be skilled and be aware of themselves in a better way. Because of this mismatch, unemployability is a bigger problem in India than unemployment. When the job market is crying out for students having good critical thinking skills, communication abilities and behavioural traits, we seem to still cling on to our old ways of learning and grading how well they have learned. Similarly, other sectors too are in dire need of our attention.

So there are real issues available for any aspiring leader or even for a person with a genuine heart to make a difference. Some of these issues, when solved, makes a massive difference and one can see the compoundable effect this has created in our country. I fervently hope that the next generation of youngsters who want to truly serve our society are willing to get their hands dirty. When this willingness goes along with a genuine heart and an enlightened mind, India will truly find its rightful place.

Dr Rajendra Prasad, president of the constituent assembly, reflected on the issue of good people thriving in our system while moving the motion for the passing of our constitution. He said, 'If the people who are elected are capable and men of character and integrity, then they would be able to make the best of even of a defective constitution. If they are lacking in these, the constitution cannot help the country. After all, a constitution- like a machine- is a lifeless thing. It acquires life because of the men who control it and operate it, and India needs today nothing more than a set of honest men who will have the interest of the country before them…It requires men of strong character, men of vision, men who will not sacrifice the interests of the country at large for the sake of smaller groups and areas… We can only hope that the country will throw up such men in abundance.'

The Future—of Us and Our Country

In a country like ours, where too often hope gives way to despair and the old ways of doing businesses are set in tone, we need a complete reimagination to re-create our future. This reimagination has to happen on all fronts and all of our existing mechanisms have to be scrutinised. The current progress that we are witnessing is on a level of small incremental changes and we seem to live by a series of *jugaads* with the occasional breakthroughs thrown in. This is also interspersed by the many crises that crop up. How do we make these breakthrough changes exponential and generate the courage to think and act big? This is a question that is right in front of us as individuals and as a society.

Many of the issues we discussed in the book, be it political, social or administrative, are deep-rooted and the young minds who come inside the system become *status-quoists* very soon. The daily wheel of the grind is so powerful, very little breakthrough is achieved by them despite the good intentions with which they enter into the system. To illustrate this, let us take the case of police reforms. The constabulary who make up bulk of the police force, approximately ninety per cent makes or breaks the image of the force by its behaviour. It's a no-brainer in management that the input variable determines the quality of the output. If we keep recruiting young men and women just after their SSLC (tenth grade equivalent) and expect them to keep performing certain critical jobs, we are setting the system up for failure. Again, the root cause in this situation is the payment of salaries and the state pays many of these resources—who are lower in the pyramid of hierarchy but important in their delivery of work—a bare minimum salary as it is already overburdened with the salary bill. This vicious cycle of poor salary combined with the low entry-level threshold attracts candidate of average quality and this will never allow the organisation to transform itself into a high-performing unit.

Change has to come from the very beginning. It has to start right from the number of personnel needed to do an optimal job (can four good guys replace seven average guys?). For a start at least, can this be experimented with and seen in a unit or should we keep playing the numbers game every time? Tinkering with the quantity and quality of our police resources goes against the conventional thinking that policemen are needed to keep up the numbers in the field and nothing else. Sadly, we seem to need them more for their numbers and not for their worth. The second question that can be thought of is this: should a police organisation keep doing all of its work by itself? In this age of hyper specialisation and role clarity, many of its daily and noncritical jobs can be outsourced including fleet management, office management and some other aspects of civilian interface. This also gives volunteers or civilian members an added incentive to take part in the governance as the police will truly start becoming public-friendly by changing from within. Several other such proposals can be brought up and thought through. Only our mind and our resistance to change stands between what is needed to be done and what is not being done.

These are not big revolutionary ideas as some might have been tried in bits and pieces but those failed mostly because of lack of sustained push that needs to be given at the top. This brings us to the question on the quality of leadership that is being offered in our country. Leadership is the single critical variable that changes the outcome more than anything. Leaders are the people who move the needle in whatever jobs they are called to perform. The current set of leaders are not very enlightened and they seem to be jaded within a short time after entering into this mighty system. Very few of them act as agents of change by setting up visionary goals and pursuing them relentlessly. Even good people, when they enter into a faulty system, get swallowed up before they realise what is happening.

This takes us to the next question about governments and their daily functioning. Without a doubt, we all agree that our governments have become very bulky and unwieldy. With multiple layers built around, our governance has also become reactionary. As these dip their fingers into all pies and make a mess, this is the right time to ask—do we really need our governments in their current form? Why are our governments ineffective? Importantly, why are our governance mechanisms faulty? What is happening to all our hard-earned money that goes in as taxes? Why is it that the services that we get are substandard and we continue to put up with those?

Let me take the two states I'm most comfortable with, Tamil Nadu and Karnataka and see where they are heading now. A simple glance at their finances will give us a picture and that is not very encouraging. For the just completed financial year 2019–20, for Tamil Nadu, the total capital outlay that is budgeted is at a poor ₹31,221 crore (out of a total budget of ₹300,000 crore) and for Karnataka it is at ₹36,930 crore (out of a total budget of ₹237,893 crore). Capital outlay is important because that is the money that is put into use for creating roads, bridges, hospitals and schools. In short, capital outlay is the money that goes into creating assets which will serve the state and its citizens. It's truly a sorry state when less than fifteen per cent of the state's expenditure goes into creating permanent assets. In fact, states spend a significant sum of their resources on managing people who run government affairs, including salaries and pensions every year. Tamil Nadu spends about ₹88,561 crore and Karnataka spends about ₹53,153 crore on them. This is equal to fifty-nine per cent and forty-four per cent of the states' revenue collection. Also, both the states, to service their current debt, allocate ₹49,700 crore and ₹28,916 crore respectively. Budgetary allocation of resources does not reflect the future growth of the state and we can see this from the poor allocation for the creation of capital assets and significant allocations for handling the historical baggage of accumulated debts and servicing those. Imagine when this is the case with two of the best states in our country one can only wonder about the other ones.

In this precarious financial condition and with the leaky infrastructure all around, the government has just become a spinning wheel that purely relies on chance to manage our daily activities and to take us from crisis to crisis with no vision of the future. It goes without saying that governments by relying on this wasteful expenditures and fine balancing of competing interests are focussing only on winning the next election. Bold reforms can really upset the apple cart and that comes with extreme risks. With the elections in India getting more into the emotional territory, there is no guarantee that a government gets elected back, if it becomes visionary (and goes against or confounds public sentiment). The last decade has shown us that common citizens are extremely pain intolerant and show their anger in the ballot boxes when their time comes. So bold reformation is no guarantee that people understand the intentions behind and support their governments.

Democracy, by its very foundation, is not a perfect mechanism to deliver the goods. As Winston Churchill said during his intervention in British Parliament during a debate on 11 November 1947, 'Many forms of Government have been tried, and will be tried in this world of sin and woe. No one pretends that democracy is perfect or all-wise. Indeed it has been said that democracy is the worst form of Government except for all those other forms that have been tried from time to time… .'[1] It's run by a group of human beings chosen by us, and anybody who comes to a position brings with them their own set of prejudices, attitudes and behaviours. The optimal stage in governance is reached when the churning happens well and the corrupt and the dead wood are weeded out through an efficient process. This should function like a well-oiled mechanism. Elections are supposed to be that efficient mechanism, but even the soul of the voter is corrupted in our country. Instead of empowering voters, we have still tied them to their identities and their limitations. They are looking for a messiah to solve short-term problems and not someone concerned about the society's ideals and aspirations of the future. This is hidden so deep inside of them that the common citizens do not even know that they really want a change unless somebody awakens them.

Without understanding the dynamics of running a government, it would be impossible to bring in reforms. Most reforms that have happened are incremental and

[1] The quote is part of a lengthy intervention by Churchill during the debate over an amendment to the Parliament Bill of 1911, which limited the House of Lords' ability to delay legislation passed by the House of Commons to no more than two years.

some bolder reforms have happened mostly at times of crises. It would also be foolish of us to wait for crises to push us to do things that we should be doing otherwise. Even if some governments start out boldly, very soon they are countered by the forces prevailing all around them. Pondering on the strong prevailing forces would take us nowhere and we need to get into an action mode with a real sense of urgency.

Also, the changes proposed cannot be academic and centralized in its decision making as people's will matters in a democracy. Governments are to reflect that will while governing the people. Because of the severe disparity around us, the societies have very severe economic and social fault lines which are only getting wider. Any act that is done for the benefit of a section of the population might severely disadvantage some other segments of the same population and alienate them. For every businessman who needs a certain relaxation in labour laws, we have millions of unorganised labourers who go to their beds hungry because of a lack of a social security net; for every extra kilometre of road that we need to build, there are Public Distribution Shops (PDS) which need better and larger quantity of rations to be supplied to them so that they can be given to the needy; for every rupee that our police department desperately needs for improved policing, there is also another department fighting for the same money and for an equally pressing issue. That's why, governance in India has become the art of balancing the impossible.

With many competing claims to the same pool of resources, what looks economically right to one eye will look morally wrong to the other. Many of the schemes to help the masses have become populist and might not do real justice to our hard-earned money that is paid as taxes. Incentives are given and thereby loyalty is earned by targeting a certain population along economic or religious lines. To change this existing structure, the language that surrounds politics itself has to change. The current language that focuses on populism, emotion and one-upmanship has to change and needs to focus instead on empowerment, empathy and enablement.

Reforms within the government need to happen at a speed and scale that hasn't happened in the history of the country. To do that we need to elect leaders who will focus on tomorrow's problems and sharpen our executive class who should do a better job of solving our today's problems. Leaders will change their narratives, only when we, the common public, change ours. When we bring all of these points to our dinner table and street-level discussions, politicians will have to change and cater to that new way of thinking. I'm certain the future generation will not forgive the decision-makers who had all the powers with them and still didn't use it for those common good because they were too worried about winning elections, getting a good transfer or criminally feathering their own nest. We need to inculcate this moral fibre into the younger generation and encourage them to aspire for a better society. To do that, many citizens with good and noble intentions have to find a way to be a part of the government, be it directly or indirectly. Sitting in our comfort zones and commenting on the state of the nation doesn't take us anywhere. It only adds to the existent pessimism. There is an opportunity for many of us to jump in and be a part of that change. The doors are open for us to contest a panchayat election and all the way to becoming an MP. There are also many other ways to run a government, from becoming an AIS officer to being a part of the states' bureaucratic system. When good, well-meaning people occupy positions of importance, it generates a speed and momentum that will be unstoppable.

It all starts with changing our belief systems, generating courage to take on the mighty forces that are deep rooted, leading our lives with a sense of purpose and finally, the understanding that the system is nothing but US—only you and me.

When we change, the system changes and when we lead, the country progresses. When we get inspired and do this, we inspire our next generation to do much better than what we have done!

That's the true measure of our worth as citizens.

ABOUT THE AUTHOR

K Annamalai, born into an agricultural family in a village near Karur, Tamil Nadu, was among the first generation to enter into an undergraduate degree from his area. He studied engineering from PSG College of Technology Coimbatore, to become a mechanical engineer and subsequently completed his MBA from IIM Lucknow. Post that, he got into the Indian Police Service (IPS) and served in Shivamogga and Karkala in his initial years and later in Udupi and Chikkamagaluru districts as district police chief. Later, he was the Deputy Commissioner of police in Bengaluru city. He quit from the IPS in September 2019 to focus on creating tangible change at the grassroots level.

Annamalai is the founder and chief servant of 'We The Leaders' (www.wetheleader.org), a foundation based in Tamil Nadu. The organisation is active in the areas of skilling and training students to improve their behavioural and communication abilities and empower rural farmers by the creation of Farmer Produce Organisation (FPO).

He is also the winner of Esprit-de-Corps award instituted by the 1968 batch of IAS officers and Sangay Lhaden Shenga award instituted by the 1992 batch of IAS officers for showing 'Exemplary Leadership Qualities' during the combined training of All India Service Officers. He is also the recipient of the Vice-President of India award during his IPS training at LBSNAA, Mussorie and SVPNPA, Hyderabad. A firm believer in the holistic and sustainable way of living, he currently farms in his home town on weekends and travels widely. He tweets @annamalai_k.